A Boyhood in the Dust Bowl,
1926–1934

A Boyhood
in the Dust Bowl
1926–1934

❀

Robert Allen Rutland

UNIVERSITY PRESS OF COLORADO

Published by the University Press of Colorado
P.O. Box 849
Niwot, Colorado 80544

The University Press of Colorado is a cooperative publishing enterprise sup-
ported, in part, by Adams State College, Colorado State University, Fort Lewis
College, Mesa State College, Metropolitan State College of Denver, University of
Colorado, University of Northern Colorado, University of Southern Colorado,
and Western State College of Colorado.

The paper used in this publication meets the minimum requirements of the American National Standard for Information Sciences — Permanence of Paper for
Printed Library Materials. ANSI Z39.48-1984

Library of Congress Cataloging-in-Publication Data

Rutland, Robert Allen, 1922–
     A boyhood in the dust bowl, 1926–1934 / Robert Allen Rutland.
        p.   cm.
     ISBN 0-87081-416-8 (alk. paper)
        1. Rutland, Robert Allen, 1922–   — Childhood and youth.   2. Okemah
     (Okla.) — Social life and customs.   3. Depressions — 1929 — Oklahoma —
     Okemah.   4. City and town life — Oklahoma — Okemah.   5. Okemah
     (Okla.) — Biography.   I. Title.
     F704.039R88   1995
     976.6'73 — dc20
        [B]   95-41936
                                                                             CIP

10   9   8   7   6   5   4   3   2   1

To the memory of "Pop"
George Albert Newman,
born Bodenham, England, 1873,
died Tulsa, Oklahoma, 1959

Contents

Acknowledgments

The patience and hard work of the University Press of Colorado editorial staff is greatly appreciated. Many helpful hands were also involved, including my sister, Mrs. Ruth Ann Bond, Lucretia Brooks Harkey, Tid Kowalski, and the Oklahoma Historical Society newspaper library staff. And how can I thank my University of Oklahoma classmate, Tony Hillerman, for his delightful introduction? Words finally fail me!

Everything is factual in this story except the fictional names given to Ben, Helen Johnson, and the rancher Potter. They were very real people whose relatives are still living, and I have changed their names in the interest of prudence and fairness.

My daughters, Betsy Farley and Nancy Rutland, were also supportive of my effort to recall some of the past, first in bedtime stories as they grew up, then in a book that shares some of the experiences of a boyhood in the dust bowl.

Introduction

About all a native of Sacred Heart, Oklahoma, can do for the memoir of a boy raised in Okemah, Oklahoma, is certify to its authenticity.

That I emphatically do. Reading Robert Rutland's recollection of how it was to be a boy in a rural world that no longer exists is like peeking over the transom into my own past. Okemah was only about thirty or so miles away from our farm. The same dust bowl winds that darkened his skies silted my mother's windowsills with dirt.

There were differences, of course. Okemah offered a higher level of sophistication. It had two blacksmith shops, movies, dime stores, soda fountains, a pool hall, a sense of daily commerce, and 4,002 residents. That might seem small to urbane readers, but it made Rutland a "town boy." To those of us who were country boys, that adds a special element of interest. We always wondered how town boys passed their time. We imagined them shooting pool, roller-skating on paved sidewalks, seeing movies, drinking soda-fountain sodas, and cavorting with those urbane town girls.

We were envious. Now, having read Rutland's remembrances, I can see that while our fantasies were poorly grounded, the envy was justified. Rutland's Okemah did, indeed, offer more variety, more opportunity, a wider choice of companions than did my own village of Sacred Heart, with its sixty-four people, one cotton gin, one church, two stores (until one went broke), and so few boys to play with that you couldn't afford to make enemies. The girls were mostly at least second cousins.

But the times and the scenery and the people were much the same. The oil fields that kept the early years of the depression more tolerable at Okemah also helped a little in the adjoining territory. Our creeks, too, were fouled with the salt water and greasy waste from the slush pits. At Okemah, Saturday was the highlight of the week, when country folks came to town to do their buying and socializing. We were those country folks at nearby (and smaller) Konawa.

We, too, lived with Prohibition. Oklahoma, Kansas, and Mississippi carried on the Noble Experiment long after the other forty-five states dropped the idea. We kids stayed out of the woods behind our farm because the local bootlegger ran his still there and didn't want visitors. I grew up, as did Bob, understanding that sheriffs took bribes and were defeated for reelection if they drove up the price of booze by arresting people. Bob and I both went from boy to man in an environment in which poverty was so pervasive that it was invisible — at least to children. At Konawa, the Saturday town for our corner of Pottawatomie County, even the privileged class (our banker, druggist, and doctor) drove used cars.

Those who share Bob Rutland's memories of the Great American Depression in one of the poorer corners of the nation may be surprised to notice the absence of any sense of deprivation. The Rutlands and their Okemah neighbors were poor folks. I'm confident they were living — as were the Hillermans — far, far below what we now call the poverty level. But the poverty index had not yet been invented. We had no ambitious political leaders teaching us that we were victims of anyone or anything. We lacked psychologists to inform us that we were losers because of childhood deprivation and family dysfunction. And so we worked on hay-baling crews for $1.25 for a ten-hour day, or made twenty-five cents an hour if we were lucky enough to get an oil field roughnecking job, and dreamed the Great American Dream, and had no notion of the privileged class until we worked our way into college and washed dishes for the fraternity boys.

I assure those of you too young to have enjoyed the dust bowl and the Great Depression that the glimpse Robert Rutland provides of growing up in the 1930s in Oklahoma is a glimpse of reality.

Tony Hillerman
ALBUQUERQUE, NEW MEXICO

A Boyhood in the Dust Bowl,
1926–1934

1

Not the Worst of Times

The sign outside town on U.S. Highway 62 read: OKEMAH/ POPULATION 4,002. My grandfather, George Newman — Pop to me — said he and I made up the "2" and that without us it would seem odd that the town had an even four thousand people. I never questioned anything my grandfather said. In 1931, when many things were being examined in America, a nine-year-old boy had no reason to doubt his grandfather's word.

Back in 1931, there was a great deal of certainty in America, in Oklahoma, and in Okemah. Okemah was still a community with a healthy outlook, even though there were a few empty storefronts on Broadway, the town's mile-long commercial street. Oil, corn, and cotton were Okfuskee County's staples, and until the depression struck, people talked more about the weather than money. The important things for a nine-year-old boy were ice-cream cones, ten-cent movies, bib overalls that seldom needed laundering, and plenty of sidewalks for roller-skating. Okemah had all those things in abundance, or so it seemed in 1931, when I became aware of worldly pleasures. To a boy born in 1922, none of the worries of the men who read the stock market pages with dread meant anything. My closest exposure to all this in 1931 was Pop's remark that my dad had lost some money in a "bucket shop," investing a few hundred dollars in something called "Cities Service." At that time, the lack of cash did not mean a denial of the good things of life.

❀

Five years earlier, in 1926, I had moved to Okemah, my presence there determined by a family conference after my father died. Circumstances decreed that I would be living temporarily, it was assumed, with my grandparents in Okemah. My grandfather had been bypassed by the prosperity of the twenties, but he still had a big house, an income, and a wife. Born in England, he was a toddler when his parents migrated to an Illinois farm around 1880. He left Illinois and moved to Oklahoma shortly after statehood in 1907. Oklahoma was hardly a decade old when he established a custom milling business near one of the county's cotton gins.

Pop had buried his first wife in Illinois and remarried fairly soon after arriving in Okemah. His new wife was Chestina E. Gorman, and the marriage apparently went wrong from the start. My mother moved out of the house as soon as she graduated from high school, then taught school for a year and married my father late in 1921. She wanted to escape Pop's drinking and her difficult relationship with Mom, as I called my stepgrandmother at her insistence. Born in 1900, my father left an Okfuskee County farm to work in an auto supply store in Okmulgee; he courted my mother while she taught school before they married. But in a few years my mother's world collapsed. My father caught pneumonia late in March 1926, died within a week, and was buried on Easter Sunday.

My father's life insurance barely paid for the funeral, leaving his wife with two babies (I was three, my sister,

Ruth Ann, barely a year old) and no money. A hasty family conference settled things — the small frame house on North Taft was turned back to the mortgage company, and my sister was sent to live with my father's childless sister and her husband on their farm near Okemah. I went to Okemah to stay with my grandparents until my mother was able to unite her family again.

Meanwhile, she went to work in an Okmulgee department store, as a five-dollar-a-week clerk in the dry goods department, and hoped to see her children often. The two-lane paved highway between Okmulgee and Okemah was a mostly straight concrete ribbon thirty-two miles long; or, as my grandfather said, "two gallons of gas and one flat tire" away from Okemah's town limits.

❁

Okemah was built on a hill settled when the government declared some Indian lands "surplus" in 1902, and auctioned off lots five years before Oklahoma statehood. Eyewitnesses said about three thousand people settled on that windswept prairie, and for a time it was a typical tent city where "drinking water was hauled in and sold for twenty-five cents a barrel," according to local historians. By 1926, Okemah had a grand, silver-painted water tower with plenty of cheap drinking water, and the tents were long gone.

Okemah is no longer a vibrant community, as it was when Woody Guthrie was born there in 1912 — a fact that many local citizens long tried to overlook. In that vanished world of the 1910s and 1920s, there were thousands of Okemahs that created a microcosm of love, bigotry, romance, hatred, generosity, and greed. Okemah and other prairie villages bore their regional characteristics proudly. Okemah was partly western, in its optimism and quick acceptance of outsiders, and partly southern, in the soft accents of its inhabitants, its prejudice against blacks, and its tolerance of booze, sidewalk fights, and public drunkenness. Okemah also maintained the old southern habit of extended credit — everything from patent medicine to flour was bought on credit, and payment was made when crops or wildcat wells came in. The exception was the J. C. Penney Company, which sold for cash only. None of this meant much to me, except that I grew up realizing how scarce cash was. The big dollar-bill currency of that day seemed large enough to cover a horse like a blanket. My world was made up of pennies, some of them Indian-heads, and buffalo nickels.

In time, I assumed Okemah was famous, for Edna Ferber had mentioned a hill called Okemah in her book *Cimarron,* which eventually found its way into my hands at the public library. Pop also assured me that Okemah was located at the end of string of hills that started somewhere up north — Coffeyville, Kansas, was his guess. South of town the lazy, shallow North Fork of the Canadian River snaked its way toward the Arkansas. North of town there was the silt-laden Deep Fork, which gave a henna tint to the hair of foolish swimmers.

When I arrived there as a three-year-old, Okemah was still regarded as a lively oil town, for it was halfway between the oil play at Cromwell and Seminole, with lots of pipeyards on the outskirts of town. Plenty of wildcatting was going on, and Sinclair and other big, integrated oil companies had busy local offices for their pipeline business.

According to *Oklahoma: A Guide to the Sooner State,* published by the WPA in 1941, Okemah was settled on government surplus land; of the three thousand people who came to the auction of town lots in 1902, a good many had stayed. By 1926, when I was taken there, my grandfather's house on Third Street had a pump in the kitchen but water came from the city lines, and a toilet and bathtub had been added to the back porch to replace the outhouse built before the city sewer system existed. All the main streets were paved, but many of the alleys were dirt roads, as were most of the farm roads leading into the judicial seat of Okfuskee County.

In Okemah itself, the main east-to-west thoroughfare, made of bricks and about fifty feet wide, was Broadway. Starting near a cotton gin close to the Fort Smith & Western tracks on the eastern end of town, the street ran about a mile and a half to the western edge, which was filled with small dwellings. To the south, about eight blocks deep, was the hilly part of town, which encompassed the school system, the Baptist and Presbyterian churches, homes of middle-class merchants, and the better homes of several physicians, car dealers, and bankers. Near the eastern edge of town a slope contained some down-at-the-heel frame houses, many of them unpainted, which were rented by transient families. It was in one of these houses that Woody Guthrie's family lived.

North of Broadway was another collection of middle-class houses, most of them built around 1918-1920, and farther north still was the town's Highland Cemetery. Perhaps it says a good deal about Okemah that the cemetery was spoken of by local folks with a good deal of pride. Ringed by magnificent elm trees, the cemetery was tended by a swarthy gentleman, Lawrence Payne, and his sons. I was a frequent visitor there because my stepgrandmother's parents were buried on the first lot closest to the entrance. The Rutland family plot was about one hundred yards further on; the grass on my grandfather Whit Rutland's grave still held scraps of artificial flowers left from his 1922 burial. My father was buried another ten yards beyond the Rutland family lots, and we dutifully tended the graves once or twice during the spring and summer. On Decoration Day, May 30, the American Legion helped us by placing a small American flag on Mom's father's grave. Mr. Gorman had been paid to come to America during the Civil War as a substitute for a drafted American. He had survived the war and migrated westward for many years until he came to Okemah around 1910, where he made concrete sewer pipes.

The fire station was on West Broadway, as well as the post office, city hall, and town library. Also on Broadway were two movie theaters, four each of grocery stores and drug stores, and several general and five-and-ten stores; the most prominent general store was the Creek Trading Company at Second and Broadway. Both the Creek store and J. C. Penney's had a string of wires from clerks' counters to the main accounting office, where cash zipped back and forth after each sale in brass cylinders. I was fascinated by their speed and accuracy and always longed to pull the cord that sent them spinning to their destination. But I never had enough nerve to ask a clerk if that was permitted.

The town had no bookstores but two blacksmiths, a cotton gin, two hotels, and a surplus of filling stations. The post office, a few steps beyond the Crystal Theater, was a town hub, and the parcel-post truck, which moved up and down Broadway, carried spare auto parts, newborn chicks, and seed corn along with the usual packages from mail-order houses. The postal truck was a Model A Ford, painted an official khaki color, with wire mesh sidepanels to protect parcels from being lost or stolen. The postman who delivered mail on foot called twice a day at all homes and businesses. The going rate in 1926 to send a letter anywhere in the country was two cents for first-class mail, and postcards were one cent.

Among the hardware stores was the one across the alley from Pop's house owned by the Box family. They seemed to stock everything that was not edible, from nails to cream separators and pocket knives to baling wire. The Boxes were an elderly couple, and they had an adopted son, a rather obstreperous boy, who bore the stigma of being a foster child. As an adopted son, he was looked upon with a mixture of condescension and suspicion by the local populace; he responded by being loud-mouthed and aggressive in the classroom and on the playgrounds. Then an accident at a baseball game turned the town from skepticism to pity. A bat slipped from a player's hand and hit the boy squarely on his forehead; he was unconscious for a time, then slowly recovered. Within a year he had resumed his belligerent way of life; but the accident had left him somewhat changed. At least he was kinder to me than he had been before, and I felt some sympathy toward him because I was, in a sense, a foster child myself.

There was another lad in Okemah, also a foster child, whose personality was similar to the Box boy's in that he was a braggart and in constant trouble on the playground. One day he came to school with some crushed wrapping paper taken from a parcel. He sought me out and showed me the address, which was in a familiar handwriting — my mother's — and written to my sister on the RFD route that Uncle Boon lived on.

"See what I found on the pavement outside the post office," he bragged.

I was curious as to how he found it and what was in it.

"It was box of candy, meant for your sister, but I found it, and finders keepers, losers weepers," he said with a leer.

"Why didn't you give it to the post office people?" was all I could say in response. The point was lost on him, and when I told Mom about the incident, she cautioned me not to tell my sister or mother, on the grounds that it would "hurt their feelings, because it probably cost a dollar and now it's a total loss."

Mom was always inclined to keep secrets. I was particularly warned not to tell my grandfather when anything extraordinary occurred. Sometimes I forgot and told him something innocuous that she had preferred to keep secret.

On the other hand, my grandfather was always forgiving. He never had any secrets, and his life was an open page for all to see, somehow endearing Pop to me in a way that still brings a warm feeling for my dear little failure of a grandfather. By 1926, he was bald, but in a bow to vanity he combed his hair forward and dyed it. He was born on February 4, 1873, although usually he was too vain to mentioned the year. He was proud of the February birthdate because it was also Charles Lindbergh's birthday, and he didn't mind being identified with the nation's aviator-hero. Pop was about five feet, five inches tall, weighed no more than 120 pounds, and his face was marked by what I would call "a good English nose." I don't recall ever seeing him wear a suit with matching coat and trousers, but neither did he wear overalls. His daily uniform was a brown or blue denim shirt, a pair of khaki-colored cotton trousers, and laced-up boots — even in the hottest weather. He sometimes paid me a nickel to unlace the boots at the end of a busy day in his grain elevator. Like most men, he wore a cap or felt hat constantly, except when eating.

Although Pop had little formal education, he was well read insofar as topics of the day went, and he had a flowing handwriting that was distinctive. He liked to draw birds on my tablets, and he taught me how to take any mark on a page and turn it into a picture of an animal, bird, landscape, or something that was at least recognizable. He also liked to teach me card games, "pitch" being his favorite because he could contrive to lose and make it look legitimate. When he was not drinking, Pop was simply a nice guy to be around. What his life would have been like had he not been an alcoholic is an idle speculation. He drank early in the day and often, to Mom's great disapproval, and thus a wall of separation existed in their home from my first days there.

Mom was probably in her late forties in 1926, and as we said when trying to speak kindly of overweight people, she was "on the plump side." She usually wore high-heeled shoes and dresses that adequately covered her full bosom. Her hair was always tinted reddish, and she wore glasses with tortoise-shell rims. To my knowledge, she never took a drink in her life, so her attitude toward Pop was always holier-than-thou and I accepted it. The anomalous situation was lost on me, even though I was aware that something called Prohibition was in effect, which meant there was something suspicious about drunks and drinking.

In Okemah there were no public watering holes for the thirsty except the drugstores, all of them with a suitable soda fountain where the clerks made sundaes, phosphates, milk shakes, and the ever-present Cokes. I loved the smell of drugstores and took to visiting them when nothing else was going on, because I could stretch out licking an ice-cream cone for thirty minutes. A single dip of ice cream, the kind made with lots of eggs and milk and flavoring, cost five cents; and if you knew the person who dipped the ice cream, you might get a bonus when he failed to scrape the dipper before plopping the chocolate or strawberry hunk on a big sugar cone.

My wonderment at the taste of ice cream increased tenfold one day when I was in a drugstore and the soda jerk announced he would give me some leftover malted milk from a takeout order. It was the most delicious thing I had ever tasted, with thick creamy chocolate that made the whole thing resemble a liquid candy bar of the best quality. But malted milks cost a quarter, and so I never had one again in all my remaining time in Okemah.

On Broadway were several cafes, most of them classified as "hamburger joints" because that was their main dish. Okemah had no outstanding restaurant, although some thought the dining room at the Okemah Hotel, run by a family of Greek descent, had merit. I never ate there, so I don't know.

There was a certain amount of "local color" in Okemah, particularly on Saturdays when thirty or forty wagons would be parked across the alley from my grandfather's mill between Third and Fourth Streets. Most of the wagons belonged to Indians who came with their teams and a blanket or two thrown in the wagon beds to join the locals for bartering, drinking, and fist fighting all day.

Okemah also had a Mexican "tamale man" who had a cart he pushed up and down Broadway every day except Sunday, selling hot tamales for five cents apiece. These were standard fare for me when Mom did not feel like cooking, and as a frequent customer I got to know Mr. Pope and his family. Pope and his wife made the tamales in his house, wrapped them in corn shucks, and then kept them in a steaming container mounted on two wheels and easily pushed from block to block. They were fat and juicy, with plenty of cornmeal encasing a peppered beef center, and they had a succulence I have never encountered since. Most small southwestern towns probably had a "tamale man" in those days, for I noticed when we were in Okmulgee or Bristow, that they had a portable tamale stand, too. If all were as good citizens as the Popes, their influence was salutary. They had two sons, both handsome, well-dressed boys, and Willie Pope's remarkable tenor voice made him welcome at our Presbyterian church when a special program was needed.

Then there were the automobile agencies on the side streets. The Chevrolet and Ford dealerships were on Fourth Street, side by side, the Buick dealer was catty-cornered from the Ford company, and a Dodge-Plymouth agency was on Broadway, between First and Second Streets. The field to select from had narrowed over the years. My father had owned an Essex, which went out of production, and my grandfather owned a Winton when I was born. By the late twenties and early thirties, the automobiles driven by the bankers, doctors, and other folks high on the social ladder were usually Buicks, with an occasional Chrysler that was conspicuous because of its rarity. One of my teachers, Alma Daniels, drove an "air-flow" Chrysler in 1934, my last year in Okemah, and it seemed to be the car of the future as she ritually drove from one end of Broadway to the other on warm nights, ice-cream cone in hand, making the U-turn as I sat on the curb wondering at the power and majesty of such a glamorous silver chariot. I saw a Pierce-Arrow once that appeared to me the longest car ever made. Most of my acquaintances' cars, however, were of necessity the more affordable Ford or "Chevy." If your family did not own a car, that meant you were *poor.*

My father was twenty-six and a personable salesman for the John Moore Tire Company in Okmulgee when he contracted pneumonia and died the spring of 1926. At twenty-four, my mother was brokenhearted and soon penniless. Her limited options were to start life anew by moving back to Okemah, or to leave my sister and me with relatives there, stay in Okmulgee, and take a job until her prospects improved. My mother was pretty, and my aunts speculated that before long she would remarry. Fiercely independent, she decided to stay in Okmulgee, see where the next turn in the road would take her, and in time reclaim her little family. Everybody understood that my residence with my grandfather was imperative but only temporary.

In 1926 my mother's father had known better days. After his first wife died, he had moved to bustling Okemah from Illinois and opened a custom milling business shortly before World War I, marrying a local belle whose husband had recently died. Piecing the story together later, I figured out that Pop and his bride early on had their differences, and he took to drinking for solace.

Pop's house on Third Street was half a block from Broadway. He probably built it around 1911, at the time my mother arrived from Illinois after living with her grandparents while Pop relocated and remarried. The architectural style was somewhere between prairie farmhouse and Victorian, and it must have been considered a comfortable place then. It had two stories with two bedrooms plus an unused, cramped boarder's room on the first floor, and two more bedrooms on the second. There was a long front porch with a swing and on the second floor a tiny alcove where I kept my toys; a play table my mother had used for dolls' tea parties as a child was also stored there. The back porch contained the added-on bathroom with a copper-coiled water heater by the commode that furnished a weak supply of hot water for the Saturday night bathers — a company that included three boarders and me. That water heater made a strong impression on me.

One winter night after using the toilet, with my overalls still down around my knees, I turned around as I stooped over. The result was that my bottom brushed the copper coils and left me branded. I cried a good deal and entreated my grandmother to send me to school the next day with a note in hand. Since I often received paddlings for misconduct, I was afraid my burned buttocks would be on the receiving end of a board unless I had a note to save me. Either I was good or my memory is slipping, for I think it worked.

By the time I arrived in 1926, the house had been painted a garish green with yellow trim. It stood out among all the whites, browns, and muted yellows on the block, but at least it was painted. Many houses in Okemah and Okfuskee County were not, including my Uncle Boon's. Early on, I understood the meaning of the southern saying that a family was "too poor to paint and too proud to whitewash."

When I came to live with Pop, he had lost his grain-milling business, but somehow he scraped together enough to build a smaller mill, covered with corrugated steel sheets, which was perched on the back of the home lot. He inhabited the house but did not "live" with my grandmother, sleeping in the other bedroom and even eating by himself. Around eight every morning except Sunday, his friends would come to the mill and the drinking would start. By the afternoon, Pop would be in a hazy world, and after supper my grandmother would often take refuge in one of Okemah's two motion picture theaters.

Despite the coolness between them, Pop called his wife "Hon" and she responded by calling him "George." It was never clear to me when the estrangement between the two took place. At times she talked about some distant past when she had been a part of Okemah's cultural scene, as a painter of china. She displayed a full set of Limoge dishes that bore her paintings of flowers and birds, and a favorite platter depicting a turkey gobbler strutting around a barnyard. I was told the china plates were brought to Okemah by a man who taught the local ladies how to decorate them, and by the time I came on the scene those dishes were her prized possessions. Most of them were displayed in a tall, glass-paneled cabinet which had a door that could be locked. This cabinet was the showplace of the dining room, and with little urging Mom would tell the story of how she had learned to be a plate artist. All her plates were signed "C.E.N.," painted in bold letters below each scene. The plates had become the hallmarks of some happier time, possibly during the first years of her marriage to Pop.

The other prominent place in the downstairs rooms was occupied by an Atwater-Kent radio, which apparently had cost a great sum of money but which proved a disappointment because reception was so poor at night that it was tolerable only at breakfast time. The one radio station we could tune in clearly was KVOO in Tulsa, which had a morning program for children sponsored by a cereal company. Each morning the radio announcer read a joke sent in by a youngster, and "Steamboat Bill" sent the winner a toy boat as a prize. I won it once with this joke:

Grandma to grandson: "I want to give you a present. Which shall it be, a cow or a bicycle?"

Grandson: "I'll take the cow."

Grandma: "I thought you wanted something to ride — you can't ride a cow."

Grandson: "No, but you can't milk a bicycle either."

End of joke and also a career in humor. I didn't even have the joy of hearing my joke and name read that day, for I didn't learn about it until I got to school and was told by my first-grade classmates that I had become *famous*.

2

Learning About Life

Prohibition was only an abstraction to any child growing up in the twenties. An exception was the short period when I noticed some of the town's lawyers and merchants limping around with a stiff leg, which Pop said was caused by drinking poisoned liquor. The noxious liquor supposedly came from Jamaica, hence the affliction was known as "Jake Leg." Before long I heard the term used more than once to describe a fool, as in "Jake-Leg lawyer" or "Jake-Leg druggist."

The repeal of the Prohibition amendment was a hotly contested issue in the first election I remember, the 1928 presidential contest between Herbert Hoover and Al Smith. Like a great many women with meager incomes, my step-grandmother had started taking in boarders, and one of the most interesting was a man who came to Okemah and placed an ad in the *Okemah Daily Leader* announcing classes in ventriloquism. How many students he enrolled was never known, but he made a strong impression because of his hand-painted necktie that depicted a foaming stein of beer over the words: Vote for Smith.

Pop was also for Smith, not because he hoped to see Prohibition end, but because he harbored a grudge against President Hoover. His rationale was that back in 1917-1918 Hoover had been in charge of the nation's wartime food supply and had caused a rigging of the price of grain.

Somehow, Pop insisted that his financial problems and the loss of his large mill was tied to "Hooverism" and thus he disliked the president. And this was even before the Great Depression struck!

Pop talked a lot about "would-be's" in government, and about the time I learned how to read a newspaper, he decided to run for the city council. He placed a small ad in the *Leader* announcing his candidacy as an independent, with a promise to keep taxes low; and the telephone rang several times the next day with endorsements from voters. I read the ad with pride, even though Mom said it was a foolish gesture and wondered how much the ad had cost. As she predicted, the election proved a disaster, as he garnered only a handful of write-in votes. I think I was more disappointed than Pop. He confided to me that some years before he had run on the Republican ticket for county sheriff and expected a large vote from black Republicans in the western part of the county. But, he recalled, the "damned Democrats" had figured out a way to challenge the blacks and had so intimidated them that he had lost the "crooked election." Perhaps this was true — Pop always seemed on the losing side, but he never lacked good excuses.

The other political events in Okemah during this period related to Leon C. "Red" Phillips, a lawyer whose offices were above the Creek Trading Company. Red was the county delegate to the state house of representatives and said to be a powerful figure. He certainly was a corpulent one, a distinction he shared with our state senator, one Nick Barry, who was owner of the Chevrolet agency as well as a banker. I thought Senator Barry was the largest man I had ever seen, and I wondered how he managed to get into one of his Chevrolets. Between the two of them, Phillips and Barry were a pair of heavyweights, giving Okemah a powerful though tiny delegation in the state legislature. But Pop was not impressed with either man and was a frequent critic.

He was not an impartial observer, however, for he seemed to hold Phillips responsible for his law partner's death through a tragic accident. To reach their office it was necessary to climb an iron stairway mounted outside the building, and if Pop's version of the accident was correct, Phillips's partner had leaned over too far while standing on the landing by their offices and fallen to his death a decade or so earlier. Or so Pop said with a scowl, intimating without any suggestion of proof that somehow it was Red Phillips's fault. Sometimes Pop's logic was pretty flawed.

Politics were a part of Okemah's routine, mainly because it was the seat of Okfuskee County. William "Alfalfa Bill" Murray was governor in 1932, and he once came to Okemah when he was making noises about running for president. All I learned about Murray was that he opposed toll bridges and had used National Guardsmen to keep the bridge across the Red River into Texas open and free. That made Murray a hero with Pop, so when Murray came to Okemah to make a speech and climbed off his truck bed to shake hands, Pop saw to it that we were in line.

What was memorable about the line was that a woman ahead of me had sharp fingernails and had scratched Murray's hand as she shook it. Murray looked dismayed as he reached for his handkerchief and said a cuss word or two about the dangers of meeting the public out in the open. He dabbed his hand and shook mine. Pop honestly believed Murray was a serious contender for the White House, so he told me this might be a day to remember.

In all likelihood, Murray's presidential candidacy was not taken seriously outside of Oklahoma, although the controversial governor went to the Democratic convention as a self-styled spokesman for the little man. Less flamboyant than Murray, but not by much, was a Democrat named Gassaway who came to town dressed as a cowboy, riding a horse with a decorated saddle and waving a white Stetson. He was running for Congress and to me seemed more like a cowboy movie star than a politician.

The other governor I remember was E. W. Marland, who came to Okemah when he was a long shot in the Democratic primary. He made a vague promise to bring a mattress factory to the town, but my strongest memory was that he looked and sounded like a stuffed shirt. At the time, Marland was trying to recoup a fortune lost in the oil business, and I was told that the familiar Conoco Oil triangle trademark was the current symbol of what had once been the Marland oil empire. That had meaning for me because all summer long I had waited for results of a Conoco contest offering thousands of dollars to the person naming their "Conoco Bronze" gasoline. How many names I submitted I cannot recall, but I was certain this contest would help Mom and Pop a great deal if I won. When the contest ended, not only was I a sore loser, but I thought their announced decision to ignore the winning name and stay with the "bronze" label was more than a little cowardly. I suspected chicanery and asked Mom to start buying Phillips or Texaco gasoline as a reprisal for such deceit.

With Pop's prejudices influencing me, I was against Hoover and wore a Roosevelt button on my overalls in 1932. After he was elected, Mom traded in the Atwater-Kent radio for a tabletop Philco, and on several occasions we listened to the new president instead of going to the movies. When the banks were closed soon after FDR's inauguration, Mom was worried about finding money to pay bills, but everyone was worried, and the crisis seemed to pass without any real change in our lives.

In those days we learned about politics in grade school, and I knew the names of our two senators in Washington — Thomas Gore and William Pine. Gore was blind, and Pop liked him. Pine had won in a fluke election, carried on the coattails of Herbert Hoover in the 1928 landslide, and he was both a Republican and an oilman from Okmulgee.

Then there was a judge in the county, John Norman, a short man who wore stiff collars and had a prominent gold watchchain ornamenting his vest. The judge was a kindly soul and according to local rumors was the richest man in the county. He drove a Buick and was never seen, even on the hottest day, in anything but a dark suit with a vest and the obligatory white starched shirt. That heavily starched shirt was his trademark.

The county official I heard mentioned most often was Wes Kennedy, the county sheriff. If Kennedy was too friendly with the bootleggers, that was only gossip. Kennedy had hired my Uncle Chris as a deputy, which made him all right in our family circle. Kennedy unknowingly provided me with my first thrill in politics. When he announced his retirement, the friends of butcher Bennie Hill, as a prank, turned in nomination papers for Hill to succeed Kennedy. Everybody thought it was a wonderful joke, until suddenly Bennie took his candidacy seriously and started to campaign. The upshot was an embarrassing defeat for Kennedy's handpicked successor. The episode turned laughter into surprise and then into a victory. I was impressed. If Bennie Hill could leave a butcher's block to become sheriff, anything could happen in a political race, even in life itself.

❁

Two resident boarders helped pay the bills for my stepgrandmother, since little income came from Pop's mill. The first was a one-eyed mechanic whose glass eye fascinated me; he had come to Oklahoma with my grandfather and was a lifelong bachelor whose only interest outside his Buick agency job was the local Masonic order. He wore a heavy mustache and had an elegant uniform in his closet that made him look like, I thought, an admiral of the fleet. The other boarder was a mysterious barber, John Pear, who was an enigma mainly because he never spoke of his past, yet gave the impression he was a man of wealth who had drifted into barbering simply because it amused him.

Mom's cooking tended toward the basic meat-and-potatoes menu. On Sundays she fried chicken, with mashed potatoes and cream gravy along with green string beans as side dishes. Her cobblers, usually cherry or peach, were memorable for their thick overlay of brown crust. Biscuits or cornbread were prepared every morning, except when one of the boarders was ailing. Then Mom offered all of us her "graveyard special," thick, store-bought white bread that was toasted, smothered in butter, and covered with milk heated to a near boil. The meaning behind the expression wasn't clear to me, so I asked one of the boarders what it meant.

"Oh, you're too young to understand," he said.

I heard that a lot, whenever I asked a grown-up a question, about half the time that was the standard answer. Only Pop, and sometimes Mom, would take the time to talk to me. I wondered if there was something most grown-ups were trying to hide, but I didn't dwell on it.

The chickens Mom fried on Sundays were often traded to my grandfather in exchange for his grinding corn or milo for a customer. A hatchet kept on a tree stump between the mill and the house was rusty because it was used only for the Sunday ritual of killing a chicken. I watched Pop perform his Sunday morning execution shortly after I came to live there, and once was enough, for the beheaded bird flopped around the backyard spattering blood over the grass and sidewalk. I screamed and cried until Mom carried me to a rocking chair and calmed me down. Thereafter, Pop was instructed to kill the chicken while I was away at Sunday school.

Except at the three mealtimes, during the day the house was quiet. The radio reception was too poor for Mom's taste, and not much social conversation took place in the house, although when Mr. Pear was absent, there was much speculation on how much money he kept in the bank or how he reportedly was "playing the stock market." I liked the mechanic but was afraid of the barber, probably because he treated my grandfather with something akin to contempt.

One Sunday when Mom was serving fried chicken, a bone caught in Mr. Pear's throat, and he coughed so hard everyone was afraid he was going to die. The clinic across the street, where Doctors Bloss and Spickard practiced, was closed on Sundays, so there was nothing to do but bundle Mr. Pear in a car and drive him eighteen miles to Henryetta, where the closest emergency room was open. When they returned late that night, Mr. Pear went to his room silently and never spoke of the incident. He was still barbering when I left Okemah, but he died not long thereafter, virtually penniless.

Other tenants had "sleeping rooms" in the house but did not eat at Mom's table. A memorable one was a Lebanese who wandered into town and started a restaurant on lower Broadway. He was about thirty and a jovial man; he told me how he had thrown his fez into the ocean when he migrated from Lebanon. He also avoided my grandfather.

Pop was a nondescript loser, by all standards of success, but he was also a nice guy. He liked to tell listeners that he was born in the English village of Bodenham, in Wiltshire, and recalled that he was almost drowned there when chased into a pond by an angry swan. Oddly, no family records existed, no Bible bore the Newman genealogy, and apparently none had been brought to America by his father. Pop spoke of brothers and sisters living in Illinois, but he kept no records of his family background, so I don't to this day know my great-grandfather's first name. All he told me was that his father left a steady job as gamekeeper for the Earl of Radnor to take his chances on an Illinois farm. He had no contact with his brothers and sisters, all older than he, and he left the family nest early on to become a telegrapher for the Chicago, Burlington, and Quincy Railroad. Then he drifted into the grain business and came to Oklahoma, seeking wealth in the new state. He built his first mill on a siding of the Fort Smith & Western Railroad when pecans, cotton, and corn were the chief cash crops of Okfuskee County.

His problems accelerated, perhaps because his marriage came apart, and by the time I came to Okemah, Pop was embittered and something of a social outcast. There were no friendly calls from neighbors, no guests for dinner, no invitations from other families. Pop and his wife seem to have been social pariahs in Okemah. My mother rarely spoke of her life as a young girl in Okemah, but it was clear that she was ashamed of her family and yearned to escape once she had a high school diploma. She spent a summer at Central State Teacher's College, and then accepted a country school post at Spring Hill, where she met my father in 1920.

I knew none of this background when I lived in Okemah. The innocence of children is a wondrous thing, for it allows them to be happy in the midst of much human misery. From my perspective, Pop's drinking left him in a jolly mood and I guessed that was why he drank. In those days, there was a great deal of drunkenness, public drunkenness, and Pop was far from being the "town drunk." Although Prohibition had long been a part of Oklahoma's history, it was hard for a youngster to understand. All I knew was that Pop and his friends drank moonshine from Mason jars or bought small bottles of vanilla flavoring (about 100 proof; or a 50 percent alcohol content!) and drank them in one gulp. The Indians who came to town on Saturday were another matter.

Officially, the law enforcement officers, including one of my uncles, were supposed to arrest drunks and stop any traffic in liquor. But not only were bootleggers living "across the tracks," but grocers knew why they hauled in vanilla by the caseload. They also knew why Indians bought "canned heat," sold under the brand name Sterno, in small tins along with a box of saltine crackers; a mound of those empty tins formed in the alley behind Pop's mill. The Indians, wearing dark, usually uncreased ten-gallon hats with their hair braided on both sides, dipped the canned heat out of the tins with crackers and ate them like an hors d'oeuvre. They would be howling drunk within thirty minutes.

One reason the Indians came to Pop's mill was that he ground a mixture of wheat and corn for them called *soufkee*. When cooked in boiling water, soufkee tasted like any other breakfast cereal to me, but the Indian men liked it mixed with a good slug of moonshine whiskey. This mixture was the Saturday special at the wagons cluttered around the mill. Those who wanted a faster and cheaper drunk went for the Sterno.

There were other stories of desperate alcoholics who drank an insecticide called Flit. My grandfather's preference was for vanilla, which cost fifty cents a bottle. Chased with corn liquor from a bootlegger, this vanilla cocktail was Pop's steady fare day after day. He paid for it by charging meager fees to grind corn and millet, by borrowing, or by selling off his few assets. And sometimes, when really desperate, he would ask me for a loan of a quarter, which he always kept track of and paid back. The word *allowance* was not in my vocabulary then, but like most of my friends I scrounged for empty medicine bottles that druggists bought for two cents apiece, for pop bottles worth the same, or for scrap metal from garages or building projects where lead and copper debris could be found.

On Saturday mornings when the Indians gathered in the wagon yard beyond Pop's mill, their wives stayed near the wagons and would eat a simple lunch of bologna and a banana, while their husbands trotted off in bands for the canned heat and crackers. There was much yelling and some fighting on Saturdays, and then at sundown the women would load their drunken cargoes in the back of open wagons, throw a blanket over them, and head for home. Later, when I heard the expression "blanket Indians," my recollection was of those silent women with their dead-drunk husbands. On Mom's advice, I stayed out of the wagon yard on Saturdays because it was the scene of so much drunkenness and fighting or yelling from early afternoon until darkness came, but I had a kind of fascination for the staggering, belligerent men with their bloodshot eyes and slurred speech.

Sometimes when the weather was good, my stepgrandmother would sit on the front porch in a swing and tell me stories until it grew dark. On many evenings, Pop would wait until Mom and I would go to the first showing at one of the two local picture shows, then he would move into the huge dining room, call the telephone exchange, and ask the operator ("Central" she was called) if she wanted to hear some music. Pop prepared for these evening exercises by drinking a few bottles of vanilla on an empty stomach. Then he would reel into the room, strum the banjo with his left hand, and rattle his "bones" with his right. Like those used in old-time minstrel shows, these were black ivory imitation bones about the size of a small pork rib, which he rattled in cadence with his banjo strumming. The racket was pretty awful. In my mind's eye, I saw the telephone operators laughing at my grandfather's drunkenness as he made a fool of himself in semipublic.

When we returned from the movie, Mom and I would slip quietly through the backdoor, move around the screened-in porch to a side entrance, and retreat to Mom's front bedroom, which was Pop's no-man's-land. I would then fall asleep on her lap, faintly hearing Pop's serenade for "Central."

As I came to understand my grandparents' estrangement, I began to feel sorry for Pop, but my loyalties were divided. Mom scrubbed my ears and sent me off first to kindergarten, then to grade school, and fed me delicious peach cobblers and pot roasts and bought me new overalls at the J. C. Penney store across the street. What does a youngster know of the misery that afflicts human hearts when he is well treated, well fed, and goes to a warm bed every night? If sparing the rod meant a child was spoiled, I was sure rotten, for I don't remember ever having a slap or spanking from Pop or Mom. At school, that was different! I was in the cloakroom pretty often and well remember my last hard spanking, administered to my rear end when I was in the ninth grade at Horace Mann Junior High. I almost cried.

Behind the house was a garden between the mill and the back porch, and Pop had planted several apple, cherry, and apricot trees beyond a frame garage and driveway on the south side of the dwelling. In the spring, Pop warned passersby who wanted to break off blossoms by standing near the garage with a slingshot, which he loaded with BB's meant for air rifles. He was able to discourage trespassers by sending a stinging BB into an unshielded rear end; when I tried to duplicate the feat with a larger slingshot he made for me out of an abandoned innertube, I had no success at all.

Pop grew potatoes in profusion by planting the seed-eyes on top of plowed ground, then covering them about a foot deep in straw. He also took pride in his tomatoes, which he fertilized with droppings from the wagon yard, along with beets and onions. Unlike many of our relatives and neighbors, Mom did not can any food during the summer; to her, the idea of canning ordinary vegetables seemed an admission of poverty, so she never did it.

❁

Okemah, like a good many towns, had blue laws forbidding Sunday entertainment, so Okemah folks, when desperately hungry drove to Henryetta to see its Sabbath movie offerings. The trip was about eighteen miles on a winding road and took the better part of an hour. On one particular night, Pop was for some reason included in our plan to visit Henryetta. What the movie was about is lost in time, but the stage show after the screening is not. A glamorous panorama of young girls in dazzling costumes kicked their highest in a chorus line that delighted Pop and me; even better was the part where the chorus girls took oranges from a box and threw them to the audience. Pop was quick enough to grab an orange for me and was a momentary hero. Even Mom must have smiled at our joy.

Perhaps the incident stands out because of its rarity, but I do remember going to a motion picture that was full of dinosaurs and other creatures, which was titled *The Lost World.* Pop coined a term for the giant lizard-like creatures, which I loved to hear him say — they were all lumped together under this word, a "dirastacutous." We joked about it many times, the word forming a bond between us because only we knew what it meant. When two people have few secrets to share, I learned they all become precious.

My stepgrandmother's penchant for secrecy was counterbalanced by her naiveté. She hoarded dollars for food but spent them readily for luxuries we could ill afford. She was an easy mark for door-to-door salesmen who knew how to flatter her or me. This was brought home when a man appeared at the front door bearing a tripod and camera. He was soliciting pictures of Okemah's most photogenic children, and he had "heard" about me. For two dollars he would take my picture and not only give Mom a copy but display the photograph along with those of other local youngsters who qualified, on Friday night on the Crystal Theater's screen.

In short order I shucked my overalls and donned the only pair of long trousers I owned, a white shirt, and sweater. Mom slicked down my hair, and I was placed on a table the photographer had moved to the front porch. He needed the light, since he had no flash device or strong incandescent lights, and with the honeysuckle on our porch

trellis as a backdrop, the picture was made. On the appointed night, we arrived at the Crystal and saw the regular show but no photographs. Mom asked at the box office and learned that the pictures had been shown the night before. She broke into tears and I had to console her, for it was a double tragedy — two dollars spent and no picture on the screen. She was slightly recovered when the print arrived, and she placed it on her dresser as her favorite photograph. Of course, I was not to tell anybody that the misadventure had cost two dollars.

Another time, while Pop still owned a slight interest in an oil lease, Mom drove us to the drilling site. Pop never drove her car, although he talked a good deal about a Winton sedan which he had owned and driven to Okmulgee in 1922 to see me for the first time. This rare family trip occurred when the well was almost ready for "spudding," or being tested to see if it was a producer. We arrived and, in time, a rumbling sound told us that something was about to come out of the ground, and it did. But what shot into the air was more brown than black, and Pop reported with disappointment that the well had hit saltwater and would be capped as a dry hole." I knew this was bad but did not understand why; such oil-field terms as "wildcat," "duster," and "tool dresser" were part of the local vocabulary and meant something to me in a vague way. Everybody understood that a "gusher" was good, the opposite of a dry hole.

When Mom took Pop on these infrequent trips, there was much banter between my grandfather and me and hardly a word spoken between them. Pop would take out his pocketknife and instruct Mom to drive close to the sunflowers lining the road. Then with a quick swipe he would cut a large blossom and in one motion bring it back into the car and hand it to me. I was impressed!

Before the depression struck, contributing to Pop's crushed spirit, I remember a Christmas Eve full of all the good things such a time should hold. Mom was too anxious to wait until Christmas morning for opening gifts, so she sent me off to church for a service that would end around 7 p.m.; the service ended early, however, and I headed for home. At the time, I still believed in Santa Claus, and as I came up the steps I could see, through the front door's large oval window pane, Pop rolling a toy car — the kind one could sit in and peddle — into the front room beside the Christmas tree. I was overjoyed and burst into the room, full of wonderment and questions about how Santa had come so early. The explanations were not satisfactory, but the blazing red "Stutz Bearcat" fire engine, complete with a bell to ring, became my favorite toy. When I saw the motion picture *Citizen Kane* a generation later, what came to mind in the final scene showing Orson Welles's innocent childhood symbol, his sled "Rosebud," was my Stutz Bearcat.

On Saturdays I showed off my new toy before my cousins and playmates. By the next spring the rubber wheels were worn down to the rim, the bell had fallen off, and a new coat of red paint was needed. During this period I saw an action-packed motion picture about fire fighting, *Five Alarm Fire,* and it made a vivid impression. Not only did I vow to become a fireman, but I spent many hours replaying the action of that movie. In my imaginary world, I was cast as the hero who saved all the children in the burning orphanage.

The fire fighter image was reinforced by the presence, two doors down from our Third Street house, of the driver of the Okemah Fire Department's hook-and-ladder truck. The house belonged to Mom's sister, so the monthly rent check was delivered to Mom for relaying to her relative in Joplin, Missouri. Each day the fire truck driver, who was reportedly paid a salary of twenty-five dollars a week, drove home for lunch, and his superiors allowed him to take the truck in case of an emergency. In short order, the heavy truck broke the sidewalk in front of the house, but the damage was worth it to see that gleaming red truck with its shiny brass fittings parked in our neighborhood five times a week.

The whole town knew when a fire was reported, for a siren atop city hall would sound its grating wail, and our driver would head off toward the smoke in a matter of seconds. The most memorable fire during my eight years' residence in Okemah was in a wholesale food warehouse, which caught fire in the middle of the night and burned to the ground before the blaze could be controlled. Along with other little boys, I rummaged through the smoldering debris later the next morning to confirm the report that the destruction had been total. As with every fire during those depression days, there were rumors of arson; Pop was always eager to spread such rumors. My Christmas fire truck had permitted me to have many fantasies about burning orphanages but none about blazing warehouses.

During my days on Third Street, my other favorite toy was a metal airplane, sturdily built, with "U.S. Army" painted on its dark-blue fuselage and red, white, and blue stars on its orange-painted wings. That toy biplane made me desire the life of an aviator, as pilots were called in the twenties. When barnstorming airmen came to Okemah and landed their planes in the hay-fields on the edge of town, I followed the crowds and went out to watch them land and take off. The charge for passengers was two dollars for a five-minute flight — far beyond my means. But when J. C. Penney's boys' department offered a stylish aviator's cap, complete with earflaps and goggles, I somehow found the money to buy one and wore it around the grade school grounds until the spectacle provoked remarks. Teasing playmates pulled it from my head and tossed it about, taunting me as I tried to recapture it. I finally retrieved it but later lost it at a movie, when I left it behind after the show ended. My budding career as an aviator was finished.

❧3❧

Kin and Other Folks

When our little family was split, my baby sister Ruth Ann was sent to live with my father's sister and her husband on a farm about six miles east of Okemah, but until she became interested in Saturday movies, we did not see much of each other. Neither my Uncle Boon nor Uncle Ray, who lived on adjoining farms, owned automobiles, so they only came to town when a neighbor, a well-to-do Creek Indian lady, offered a ride in her roomy Buick. Uncle Boon and Aunt Ethel lived in an unpainted, two-story frame house that sat atop a hill about five miles northeast of Okemah on a county road. It had a well outside the kitchen door, an outhouse about thirty yards to the east, and a henhouse that provided plenty of fried chicken on special days.

No electric lines ran to the house. Heat came from the blackjack oak trees chopped and split on the farm, and light was supplied by kerosene lamps. The closest telephone was about a mile away.

When my sister was old enough to attend grade school at Spring Hill Elementary, she either walked two miles or rode the gentle stallion "Old Baldy" in bad weather. Oklahoma's farm roads ran along section lines enclosing 640 acres; they were strictly dry-weather roads, and the road to Uncle Boon's was a quagmire when it rained — chains were helpful but no guarantee of keeping a car moving forward — and the likelihood of getting stuck might have given Uncle Boon an excuse for his carless status. He once owned, briefly, a Model A Ford but usually depended on Mrs. Brooks for rides into Okemah on Saturdays unless it rained, for once the roads were covered with water, it was easy to get stuck in the mud. Chains were a part of every motorist's equipment, as well as kits for fixing flat tires. Most roads in Okfuskee County were covered with gravel or simply graded dirt roads with not many drainage ditches. When we went to Henryetta or any other town, Mom stayed on the paved highways; when a tire went flat, she would stand on the roadside until a gentleman stopped to fix it — a stratagem that never seemed to fail.

My father's oldest brother, Ray, was seldom seen in Okemah, but in family circles he was talked about a great deal after one of his boys wrote a few hot checks and signed his father's name to them. This cousin was a handsome guy but too fun-loving; Ray rescued him several times by paying off the bad checks, but then stopped warning him and let the law take its course. The cousin was sent to the state penitentiary at McAlester and his name only mentioned in hushed tones. I had the feeling that Ray's stern attitude was dictated only by the fact that he could barely keep up his mortgage payments, and he was not trying to teach a lesson so much as he was trying to stay solvent. But I suspect that my Aunt Lulu's heart was broken, and the subject was never alluded to by any uncle or aunt at family gatherings. In time, this errant young man was known simply as the "black sheep," and I soon learned that every family has at least one, sometimes several; most of them had some lovable quality that endeared them to the more solid side of the family.

Family is family, but when my Uncle Chris, a deputy sheriff, came to the house one day asking for Pop, I was instinctively afraid something was wrong. I told him Pop was out in the mill, then through the back window I saw him escort Pop toward the alley. My uncle had jailed Pop on a charge of public drunkenness because in an ill-advised moment Pop had bought a used car on credit and driven it home, or rather, had weaved the car through town into the backyard. Somebody had complained, so Pop was in jail until nightfall. He came home amidst much crying by Mom, the car disappeared, and I heard Aunt Kate explain that the only reason her husband had jailed Pop was that somebody had lodged a complaint. I seemed to be the only one who had hard feelings toward my uncle about the incident.

Okemahans who did not drink vanilla or bootlegger whiskey or listen to their radios gravitated toward either the Crystal or Jewel Theaters several times a week. For Mom they were not a source of entertainment so much as a refuge and a way to escape from her unhappy life. The Crystal was owned by a Mr. Burke, an older man with gray hair and a hawk-like nose. If you came before the movie started, a large painted curtain greeted you, displaying several young women standing on a Greek porch and dressed in filmy gowns. The music played while we waited was invariably the mournful "In a Monastery Garden," which I grew to like.

Thursdays were Buddy Night at the Jewel, which meant a two-for-one admission price; by waiting until you saw a man without a lady, you could ask to be his "buddy." I saw a movie every Thursday night, even if Mom did not go, and I was usually home by my nine o'clock bedtime.

The Jewel Theater was owned by the Slepka family and was smaller than the Crystal. When I first started going there, a decorated sign would flash on the screen: NO SPIT-TING. $5 FINE! Some patrons ignored the sign, but I never saw anybody arrested. One night a brazen scofflaw worked on a huge wad of chewing tobacco and let go into the uncarpeted aisle about every five minutes. Mom moved us back, out of his line of fire and away from the smell and spray, but I was fascinated by his aim and capacity. Ordinarily, I fell asleep before the first reel was screened.

The Jewel's stage curtain depicted the main street of a large city and was not in the same class as the Crystal's idyllic scene. Both were among the first businesses in Okemah to install air-conditioning to replace the ceiling fans that had whirled overhead from spring to fall. Since movies were only a quarter for adults and ten cents for children, Mom justified the expense by saying that a fifty-cent bottle of vanilla would pay for two movie tickets.

Vanilla was not always allowed by Pop's meager cash intake. Bootlegging was commonly practiced, and the clear, colorless corn liquor offered more raw alcohol for less money. One hot day, after I had been playing cops and robbers with my friends, I ran into the kitchen where Pop was standing near two of his drinking buddies. There was a clear glass of liquid on the table, and I drank it in a single gulp, assuming it was water. Within seconds I became sick and threw up, to the dismay of both Pop and Mom. By then I was about the only common concern they shared, and Pop promised he would keep his drinking buddies out of the kitchen after that. He built a lean-to beside the mill, found an iron cot and a hotplate, and spent his evenings there after the corn liquor incident.

That situation lasted for months; I saw how lonely Pop was and tried to spend more time with him at the mill.

He became more reclusive, too. Because shooting a gun in town was not forbidden, on Sundays he would sit on the mill's front porch with his .22 rifle and take shots at pigeons that gathered in flocks around the wagon yard, feeding on the grain dropped by horses on Saturday. He would shoot a couple and clean them for his supper, which he cooked on his hotplate stove.

Pop also liked to eat the crawfish I caught in a large pond on a dairy farm east of town. By crawling under a barbed wire fence, I could escape the mean bull that often seemed to be on guard, and by using a piece of bacon, catch forty or fifty "crawdads" in a quick, dip-and-haul-out exercise. The trick was to tie the bacon securely to a piece of string, then dip it into the shallow water where the crawfish swarmed. They grabbed the bacon and before they released their grip, I hauled them out and into a bucket. Pop's eyes would light up when I brought a mess of crawfish back to empty into a boiling pot. He said they tasted like shrimp, but they didn't agree with me, so he ate them all with relish.

Pop's total banishment ended when a swarthy stranger named Ben came to him and asked for work. Pop offered him a room in return for his labor, and in short order Ben moved into the lean-to and began to tinker with the machinery, which was going to ruin because of poor maintenance. Soon Ben was running the mill, leaving more drinking time for Pop and his cronies, men who swore a great deal except when I came around.

I didn't like these men, not only because they swore but also because they talked about women, even though in my innocence most of their remarks meant nothing to me. But one day as I approached their meeting place, I heard one say he had done something that sounded pretty awful to me, something vaguely but certainly evil, and he had done it with his mother-in-law. Now, for sure, I didn't like him, and when he was later accused of arson and became a laughingstock of the town for his bungled job, I was secretly pleased to hear of his blundering.

My feelings for Ben were different. He was the mysterious stranger who drew sidelong glances from customers in the mill, but Ben was always kind to me. He kept to himself most of the time, and we heard he had run away from his home "back East someplace." We had a large apricot tree in the backyard, which I would climb and pretend to be in Africa, looking down on lions and tigers that could not reach me. Perched up there one warm summer day, I saw Helen Johnson drive down the alley, park her car, and go into Ben's lean-to. Later that evening, I heard laughing out there, and the next morning I found two empty prescription bottles marked "Paregoric" near the door. The bottle smelled of licorice, which I dearly loved to chew, so I asked Mom what paregoric was. She said it was "dope," and the manner of her explanation told me that something wrong had been going on between Helen and Ben. I didn't pursue the matter, but I looked for the prescription bottles they threw away since they had a cash value of two cents at the drugstore. I had no other knowledge of what dope was — it was just *bad!*

This was the era before people worried much about body odor, since smells around the wagon yard were an accepted a part of life. But Ben (who seemed old to me, though he was probably thirty-five at most) hardly ever bathed in our tub and had a beard stubble most of the time. He also dipped snuff, and usually had a trickle of brown juice on his chin. I couldn't figure out why a pretty young woman like Helen Johnson would be spending time with him. Helen's dad owned a lumberyard, she drove a new Buick, and was "not bad-looking" as we said in a back-handed compliment.

Helen came back a few months later and saw me.

"Have you seen Ben?"

I remembered those empty bottles and told Helen I hadn't seen Ben all day.

"Tell him I came by, will you?"

I promised I would, but in a matter of hours it was evident that Ben had left his lean-to room without a note and with all his belongings strewn about as though he was away temporarily. He never came back, however, and for many months whenever I ran into Helen by chance on the street, she would always ask about him. This was my first encounter with the mysterious ways of men and women, and it troubled me. In those days we called people who used drugs "dope fiends," and I asked Mom if Ben was such a creature. She dodged that question and others I asked about the relationship between Helen and Ben. I sure didn't want to grow up to be like Ben, but I wondered why a pretty young woman with lots of money would want to be alone in that dirty shack with such a strange man. That's a mystery I still haven't solved.

I was somehow troubled by the coolness between Mom and Pop; after all, they were married and supposed to be loving. Yet in time I realized that Pop and Mom were hardly speaking, even though he still spoke to her affectionately when they were by chance in the same room, which was a rare happening.

As the Ben and Helen incident passed, I became involved in the mysteries of sex myself. Two sisters who lived at the other end of our block asked me during a morning of cops and robbers if I would go into the garage behind their house to play. The next thing I knew they were telling me to pull out my penis, and the older sister was asking me to touch her between her legs. Of course I did as I was told, then was instructed by them that since we had done something very naughty, I must never reveal our secret to anyone. Okemah had so many secrets!

Their warning threw me into a quandary of conscience, and that night at bedtime I began to cry. When Mom asked what was wrong, I told all. Well, she explained to me, that didn't hurt anything because I was too little to know what those mean girls were talking about. I felt much better then and still am grateful for her gentle way of telling me that children aren't accountable for rules meant only for their elders.

"Jesus loved children, and he won't hold this against you," she whispered. All my guilt suddenly disappeared. As she held me and rocked back and forth, Mom seemed to have the power to make everything seem purposeful. My first encounter with sex had happened to make me more careful around girls — at least that was the way I read her meaning.

Mom had the answer to so many problems and questions; at times, however, her solutions were not practical. She tried to save gasoline at sixteen cents a gallon by pressing the clutch pedal to the floorboard when driving down a long hill. Milk in the icebox often spoiled because we skimped on cakes of ice (twenty cents each) to save money. The lights were never left on in an empty room, and the same rule applied to gas stoves. Light bulbs were frequently moved from socket to socket.

Money was so hard to come by. How we survived was never clear to me, for the mill produced a tiny income and the two boarders and occasional roomers must have provided only a meager weekly payment. The only other money coming in was from the rent on two houses in the next block, which Mom had inherited from her father. He build them during the boom times when there was a great deal of drilling for oil in Okfuskee County. Pop's mill produced a dollar here, a half-dollar there, and that was only drinking money.

After the depression set in, the big oil companies pulled out, but Okemah merchants kept going with an economy limping along on poor crops of cotton and corn. Bills from the grocery store or bakery were settled once a month, if possible.

Owning a new car was Mom's dream. Her old Chevrolet had smooth tires, a weak battery, and a bad paint job. Prospects for a new car were bleak when suddenly a rumor swept through town about a pipeline crew coming for a big job. In a few days, my Aunt Kate came by and arranged to help Mom cook for the pipeline crew. Our dining room was converted overnight into a boarding hall with three long tables covered with white oilcloth that was easily cleaned with the swipe of a dishrag. Aunt Kate came about 5 A.M., and the biscuits, bacon, eggs, and hot coffee were ready when the crews arrived at 6 A.M. They took sack lunches prepared by Mom and my aunt to their job, and returned about 6 P.M. for supper. Mom arranged credit from the butcher, baker, and grocer, with the understanding that when the pipeline company paid her, they would have her check. She joined Aunt Kate each morning and spent most of the day baking cobblers and roasting pork or beef in the single gas stove; it was never allowed to cool before the last cup of coffee was poured about 7 P.M.

The pipeline crew soon professed a partiality for Aunt Kate's cobblers, which she baked in deep pans and ladled out after generous servings of pork chops, or a beef roast, with plenty of helpings of green beans and mashed potatoes. They washed the food down with gallons of coffee, mostly black and plenty strong.

Mom talked a good deal about what she would do when the pipeline company paid her, and I decided to make some money too. I made a tent out of an old but clean handkerchief and placed inside this canopy my favorite toys — a lion and elephant made out of what was then called "celluloid" — and charged the pipeline men a nickel to see my circus. The well-fed crewmen were in good spirits, and five cents didn't seem to matter to them.

Along with my sporadic sales of empty bottles and scrap metal, my circus venture seemed to prove that I had some idea of how the free-enterprise system worked, and it gave me a false sense of success. Later, when I tried selling the *Saturday Evening Post* or *Collier's* for five cents to stores and barbershops on Main Street, I found out how big a nickel could be. And I also learned about competition, for another youngster named Amos Maxwell, supposedly a go-getter of the first order, was ahead of me most of the time. I was making sales only through luck rather than enterprise, and after some months of sending back the covers of unsold copies of magazines, I lost my early confidence to despair. Not only had I made no profits, but the Curtis Publishing Company notified me that I was nearly a dollar in arrears. A few weeks later I received a "dun notice" and had to have the meaning explained. On Pop's advice, I decided that a big Philadelphia outfit was not going to send me to jail, and besides I had sent the covers back and they must have been lost in the mail. I still felt uneasy, however, until the Curtis company bookkeepers gave up on me as a bad risk.

Another money-making scheme backfired when I tried to make some cowboy chaps out of rubber inner tubes. The large ones from truck tires were roomy enough for a small boy's legs, and with some brads and watercolors I devised a makeshift pair of imitation cowboy chaps that impressed my peers. One offered me a quarter to make him a pair, but when I was unable to duplicate the original pattern, he objected and paid me only a dime for my trouble. Not long after this default on a contract, I was trying to become a Cub Scout, and one of the rites of passage was to put on boxing gloves and take on a fellow Cub. My fate placed me in the ring (actually a mat in the basement of the First Baptist Church) with the same boy who thought my chaps were unsuitable. He was a couple of years younger but a real scrapper, and in short order he had me terrified by his energy and punches to my ears and eyes. If he wanted revenge, he had it that night.

Another learning experience with Cub Scouts came shortly after the boxing-ring humiliation. A Cub Scout rally was held at the football field where I often watched the Harjos and Tigers excel. The competition was for blue ribbons that winning teams attached to the pack's totem pole. My team's assignment was to push, with head down like a butting billy goat, a softball from the starting line to two croquet wickets crossed like an X (from above). Simple enough, except that I got confused when the instructions were handed out. I thought the point of the game was to push the ball all the way through the wickets, so I scrambled along on my knees, pushing the ball for all I was worth to my teammates' mild cheers.

To my dismay, my last shot was weaker than I had planned; instead of going though the wickets, the ball stopped dead center in the middle of the X. While I was thinking I had failed, one of the scorers said, "Gosh, that's perfectly in the center, no need to measure this one." The other official scorer said (in effect):"You're right — this is the one to beat." Amid yells from my fellow Cubs, I realized I'd done something my peers were applauding, but the truth was, I had done the right thing by mistake.

Later, when I placed my blue ribbon on the totem pole, I kept mum on my secret. But there was a lesson learned: Try as hard as you can, and somehow, even when you think you've lost, you still might win.

A popular song at the time, meant to buoy the spirits of the American people then living on hope, was "Happy Days Are Here Again." Mom said that when the pipeline company paid her, there would be happy days in our house. While we waited for the check to come, Mom and I drove one day to Aunt Kate's house on the west end of town. As we were returning, the engine began to sputter and cough. Mom began pulling and pushing on the choke, until suddenly, with a great gasp, the car leaped forward into an intersection on Fourth Street just as a Willet Whippet whirled in front of her car. The impact threw the smaller car over the curb, and it landed on its roof.

Mom screamed and I began to cry, but our shouts and tears turned to joy when a young man emerged from the wreck unhurt. He admitted he had been speeding because he was late for work, and he held Mom completely blameless.

"In fact," he volunteered, "I don't think we even need to tell the police about it. I'll just send a wrecker over to have my car hauled out of this man's yard, and we can forget all about it." This was in 1927 or 1928, when life was handled by a spirit of give-and-take. Mom was happy to leave it that way, since she had no insurance whatever. The incident was closed.

Except for the green paint on her front bumper, Mom had no reminder of her accident, but she yearned all the more for word from the Sinclair Prairie Pipeline Company. When the check came at last, she went to the Chevrolet dealer and bought a sporty cabriolet model that looked like a convertible but actually had a hard top. The car was a stunning change from the black and brown models of that day, for it was painted glossy sea-green that made your heart leap at its beauty. Mom drove it up and down Broadway for a few weeks to make sure that everybody in town knew she had a new car; for a little boy it was another lesson learned: There is nothing so elevating to a person's morale as the purchase of a brand-new car.

Another of Mom's purchases was less successful. Again, a caller at the front door was involved. On a cool spring morning a well-dressed man twisted the bell, and I answered the door. He held a large bag and asked to see the "lady of the house." The man was invited into the parlor, and he told an amazing story as he pulled a fox fur-piece out of the bag. The fur was, he admitted, stolen and had been handed to him by a no-good cousin to repay a debt. He could not turn in the cousin but didn't need the fur, so he would sacrifice it for ten dollars if Mom would keep her mouth shut.

Poor gullible lady, she had some of the pipeline money left, but was hesitant. He pressed his case, saying time was running out. He would take eight dollars. In moments the deal was done, the eight dollars counted out, and the stranger disappeared.

The following day one of Uncle Chris's fellow deputy sheriffs appeared on the front porch with a lady who seemed very agitated. Where was my grandmother? She came out directly, and the deputy told her the lady's fur had been stolen and seen in Mom's possession. There was much crying — Mom was a superb crier at every semicrisis and a blubbering one when a real problem arose — and the deputy said if the fur was returned no further questions would be asked. In five minutes the episode ended, and I am fairly sure that Mom never realized that she was the victim of a criminal scam. She wanted to forget it as soon as possible. The loss of eight dollars was on her mind for ages, but the fur salesman was never mentioned again.

Somehow Mom heard that a reclusive gentleman living at the Elk's Home in Okmulgee was paying high prices for tinfoil, the popular name for the thin sheets of aluminum (sometimes bonded to paper) used for packaging cigarettes, candy, and other products. How much did he pay? What was his name? Mom did not know, but she began saving tinfoil in a ball that grew by the day. In short order, tinfoil collecting became compulsive. Big money, she was convinced, was involved.

Taking all this on faith and instructed by Mom, I began to strip tinfoil from discarded cigarette packs, Hershey bar wrappers, and other trash found around Pop's mill. Conscientiously, I looked for Lucky Strike, Camel, Chesterfield, and other cigarette packs thrown away by the foolish smokers who had no knowledge of our secret.

The process went on for months, until the summer of 1931, when the hoard was about the size of a softball and weighed perhaps two pounds. Mom kept this treasure on the buffet in the dining room, near her Limoge platter that bore the turkeys she had painted long ago. The exercise came to an end sadly, however, when Mom's only lady-friend, a widow with henna-red hair like Mom's, noticed the odd-looking lump of crumpled wrappers.

"What," she said in astonishment, "is *that?*"

Mom explained and seemed a bit nervous about the identity of the potential buyer.

"Golly," her ladyfriend said with a laugh, "I didn't know anybody still fell for that crazy story." She then proceeded to tell Mom that the whole thing was a "silly hoax," which I assumed meant it was all a lot of hot air. Mom, of course, began to cry.

"It's worthless, honey, I'm sorry to say," her friend said in consolation.

A week or so later, Mom tossed the ball of tinfoil in the trash. Her only comment was, "I don't know who starts these silly stories anyway!"

Mom never seemed to learn from her bad experiences. One day a door-to-door salesman came into the parlor to demonstrate an electric machine he was selling that was a cure-all for backaches, headaches, and assorted other common ailments. The machine, when plugged into the wall socket, emitted a crackling noise as a blue electric spark passed between two terminals. The idea was to hold two black handles as the current was passing through, and the affected parts of your body would be relieved by the electric sensation.

How much Mom paid for this charlatan's device I cannot remember. She tried it a few times, then hid it out of sight in the dining room cupboard. I never saw it again.

❧4❧

A Melting Pot — of Sorts

Okemah, in those days, was one of the southern towns where black people were not welcome after dark. No blacks lived in town, except a few servants; on Saturdays, however, black farmers came into Okemah for food, overalls, shoes, kerosene for their lamps, and an ice-cream cone or bottle of soda water. The whole concept sounds insane in the 1990s, but in that era the color line was so deeply embedded in the southern social order that few questioned its existence and still fewer its injustice.

After the proceeds from my circus tent show disappeared, and no prescription bottles were to be found, I needed income. After negotiating a one-dollar loan from Mom, I opened a "pop stand" near the wagon yard where there was a steady flow of blacks and Indians on Saturdays. A case of twenty-four bottles of grape or strawberry soda water cost sixty-five cents, a cake of ice to keep the bottles cold cost a dime, and the rest of the dollar was needed for change. At five cents a bottle, the potential profit was forty-five cents on a case, if you didn't drink up any of the inventory.

The summer heat made my stand a success from the outset. My favorite customer during that blistering summer was a black man called "Whistlin' Bill" because of the *s* sounds he made, owing to a large gap between his two front teeth. He brought his corn to Pop's mill to have it ground into cornmeal, and while the grinding took place, Bill would buy a bottle of my grape soda pop. Bill wore bib overalls, as did most of Pop's customers, and his straw hat was drenched with honest sweat. I loved to hear him talk, for his conversation was almost a melody when he ran into a string of *s* sounds.

One scorching afternoon, when the thermometer seemed to soar by the second, Bill sought the shade of my soda-pop stand, bought two bottles and drank them down, one right after the other. None of my other customers ever seemed able to afford two bottles, and Bill's tattered overalls and excessively worn shoes led me to believe he was living on an extremely limited income. Pop reassured me, however, that Bill was not living beyond his means.

The pop stand was a successful venture, but eventually it became boring as the weekday customers became fewer and fewer. The Indian women never spoke, indicating their choice by a nod, and they drank in silence, handed back the empty bottle, and returned to their wagons or the shade of an enormous cottonwood tree that flanked the wagon yard. In truth, I longed for more customers like Whistlin' Bill. Bill was such an easygoing man that I thought everybody knew and liked him. How much of a burden he bore from being black and poor was never revealed by that remarkably cheerful human being.

The other memorable black who came to Okemah on Saturdays was a tall, spindly lad of ten or twelve who had been born without arms. One early spring Saturday he came into town and waited around the alley by the Jewel Theater; this was a favorite spot for the many marble games played "for keeps," the outlet for gambling if one had the marbles and the courage. This superb marble player took on all the white challengers, who were confident they could keep up with an armless black youngster. His total garb was a worn pair of overalls, and he was barefooted; besides his obvious handicap, the boy's demeanor was deceptive until the play began. The whole point of marble playing was to knock marbles out of the ring and then they were "keepers." A fairly harmless form of gambling, it became an intense sport when the black youngster used his big toe to send his "taw" hurtling into the mass of marbles at great speed. As long as one marble went out of the ring, he would continue to pop others out; and in a few minutes he could usually clean out one white boy's marbles, then go on to the next victim.

At the time, I understood nothing whatever about social mobility, but it was pretty clear to every spectator and victim that blacks often were able to show their superiority in one-on-one contests. Older whites and blacks would stand back and marvel at the boy's uncanny confidence and his use of his toe. I was never a victim because I was too little and too scared to take on a champ. He was only in Okemah for one spring, as I recall, but he left his mark on me as the first severely handicapped person I had encountered who made his way without asking for any favors.

The other blacks seen in Okemah came every Armistice Day, November 11, from the state reformatory for young blacks at nearby Boley. Boley was one of those southern towns founded by Negroes, for Negroes, and peopled only by Negroes, thus it had not grown up naturally over time. The *WPA Guide* reported that Boley was named for the roadmaster of the Fort Smith & Western Railroad, and its location was chosen because "much of the surrounding area had been allotted to Negro freedmen listed on the rolls of the Creek tribe at the time of the division of the Indian lands."

Okemah, as the county seat, was the focal point for such major events as the Armistice Day parade, which featured the black drum-and-bugle corps from the reformatory. The band had a marvelous jazz beat and was arrayed in surplus World War I khaki uniforms that made the bandsmen appear to be juvenile counterparts of the doughboys of 1917-1918. They marched behind a small black drum major, and since I was also a kind of runt, I could sympathize with him as he strutted down Broadway ahead of a well-rehearsed band with a loud brass section. The rumor was that he was serving time at Boley because he had killed his grandmother in a family argument. Even though no one knew the truth of the story, it was assumed to be true and repeated as such at every corner of Broadway, as the band marched and the drum major pranced to their jazzed-up version of Sousa's marches.

The only other incident I remember that involved blacks during my Okemah days was the shooting of a Negro man on the Okfuskee courthouse steps. I had been playing with my pals when somebody rushed into our group and said, "Old man Potter just killed a nigger on the courthouse steps!" We all immediately ran the three blocks to the courthouse to see if the victim was still around, but the body had been moved, and a custodian was there with a pail of water, mopping up the blood.

I knew who Potter was because he had come to Pop's mill once to pick up some feed; he told me then that if I came to his ranch, he would let me ride a pony. Months and years went by and we never went to Potter's ranch, but I kept hoping that somehow I could take him up on his offer. After the shooting incident, however, I lost interest. The dead man had worked for Potter, and the story was that he had assaulted Potter in a drunken rage; then Potter threw him into a car, making a "citizen's arrest" with the aid of a .38 pistol he buckled on with a holster, and headed for Okemah. Potter claimed that the black man tried to take the gun away on the courthouse steps and that he had been forced to pull the gun and kill him in self-defense. I heard no more of the story, but justice for blacks was so rare in those days, we all know how it ended.

❧ 5 ❧

Lessons — in School and Out

Fighting and violence were common in Okemah in the twenties and early thirties, as were run-ins with the sheriff. Saturday nights were a time for blowing off steam, but I was isolated from bloody noses and ripped shirts while we still lived on Third Street. For a time it seemed that what went wrong around our house was related to either the "Hoover Depression" that Pop alluded to so often or the weather.

Except when it's snowing, children can be oblivious of the weather, but in the early 1930s nobody could overlook the searing summer heat or the spring dust storms that rolled in from the West. The red-tinted clouds churned and could be seen at a distance, then the grit-filled air surrounded everything. When the first one came to Okemah, Mom called me inside and we watched from the dining room windows as people outside bent their heads and walked into the wind. Mom had the windows closed, but the dust crept in through cracks insidiously; in a few minutes tables, floors, and kitchen counters were covered with a thin, reddish grime. The winds would last until the sun went down, and the next morning was usually clear and bright, all the more beautiful for its freshness. Then the routine of dust cloth and mop brigades would be seen all over town.

Rain, or rather the lack of it, was also a topic forced into every conversation. During those summers of intense drought, where long dry spells were punctuated with random dust storms, the newspapers began to tell us how many days had elapsed since the last rain. Corn and cotton suffered, which meant that the hard-pressed farmers and merchants were bound to have rougher times.

Mom speculated that we were being punished by God, and I believed her. A vacation Bible school was being held at the First Christian Church, and although we were Presbyterians, I enrolled in the hope that some good would come out of my associating with other souls and learning about the Good Book. The classes emphasized rote learning the titles of the sixty-seven books in the Old and New Testaments. Although I learned how to memorize in an era when such a skill was considered useful, I did not learn much about what the Bible contained or — to my great disappointment — why God was punishing us with the heat waves and dust storms. What I did notice, and it stuck in my mind, was that we never seemed to have dust storms on Sundays. So I was convinced that there was a divine plan was at work.

Sundays were always special, but particularly so for me, because at least once a month my mother would come to visit me then, on the only day she wasn't clerking in the Okmulgee department store. I never knew which Sunday she might come, and one Sabbath when I went to the schoolground to play I missed her visit and cried as only a broken-hearted child can. I adored my mother, thought she was the most beautiful woman in the world, and was so anxious to see her that after this mishap, I stayed around the house after dinner every Sunday, hoping to see her boyfriend's car, a dark-green 1932 Chevrolet with a rumble seat and two-tone stripes, pull into the driveway.

When my mother visited Okemah, a regular ritual was to visit the Palace Drug Store for an ice-cream cone. I liked going to the drugstore for a treat because I wanted other boys to see my pretty mother and admire her, too. Sometimes she came empty-handed, but she usually brought me a toy car or lead soldier. We went for an ice-cream cone, and then she was gone.

At nine o'clock Sunday mornings, I walked a block to the Presbyterian church for Sunday school. The local Presbyterian congregation could not afford to pay a minister, but volunteers ran a Sunday school, and even though our numbers were small compared to the large Baptist, Christian, and Methodist congregations, we thought it important to say the Lord's Prayer the "right way," that is, "And forgive us our *debts,* as we forgive our *debtors.*" That was the only difference I could see between the Presbyterians and the other sects, for the words *grace* and *predestination* had no meaning for me.

Probably the reason why the Presbyterian church could stay open, even though too poor to have a minister with a Sunday sermon, was that a wealthy family in Okemah contributed for the upkeep of the building. The Sunday school principal managed the J. C. Penney store; he was a handsome man with slick, reddish hair whose wife taught my Sunday school class. She had to keep discipline because of an intense rivalry in the class between two brothers, who managed to make life miserable for me during the weeks at kindergarten and again at Sunday school. There was no escaping them.

One Sunday morning before classes began, the older of the two asked me what I knew about birds. "Do you know the wingspan of a crow?" he asked.

The matter of a crow's wingspan had never claimed my attention, but I didn't want to seem ignorant that morning, so I hazarded a guess of twelve inches and hoped I was close.

"Huh, that's all you know! Some crows measure three feet from wing tip to wing tip," he said with a sneer.

With my stupidity so apparent, I welcomed the arrival of our teacher. She was usually pressed to keep us quiet for longer than five minutes and read stories from the New Testament that kept our attention. I liked best the ones about Noah's Ark and the baby Moses being found among the bulrushes. She once asked us to memorize a verse from the New Testament, but gave up after we lazy youngsters showed no talent in that direction. I was the laziest of all, for I knew that the shortest verse in the Bible was John 11:36 — "Jesus wept." When I fell back on that, my teacher rolled her eyes as if to say that I was beyond all hope, but she said nothing. In my shame, I was grateful for her lenience.

After class the churchgoers reassembled for a final parting prayer and hymn. We all watched the posted figure telling how much was collected for the day, and I don't recall that it ever reached ten dollars *total.* Mom saw to it that I always put a nickel in the plate, which was the usual contribution from all my fellow students. A half-dollar was a rarity, while any currency in the plate excited much speculation about who had that kind of money.

One Sunday after the service, I stepped in front of a car parked by the curb. The driver was a bit careless and started forward just as I stepped off the curb, but the car moved so slowly that I was simply pushed into the space between its bumper and radiator, startled but unharmed. A woman's scream caused the driver to apply his brakes, and after much ado over the incident, I was allowed to proceed under my own power to prove nothing had been broken. I strutted home like a cat that had eight lives left.

Despite my shortcomings as a biblical student or my fidgety times in the Sunday school, I did learn to pray in that little church, and the Sunday afternoon waits for my mother became so important to me that I began to pray every night, asking God to "please let me go live with my mother" someday. The intensity of my prayers increased when my mother moved from Okmulgee to Tulsa in 1929.

Long before that happened, however, I found a main interest in life outside the home on Third Street. An effort to start a kindergarten paid for by private subscription had succeeded, and at five I was sent to a makeshift school in the old American Legion hut on West Broadway, where I learned how to count, read, and fight. The fighting was with those pesky brothers who somehow saw me as a rival, even though I was very short and not good at fighting. Maybe it was my crying that attracted them, but I remember that on a warm spring day one of the brothers held me down and the other hit my face until my nose started bleeding. That was the first of many bloody noses, as a bully was always in the background in those days.

Blessed relief came, nevertheless, for we children did not hold grudges. This was apparent when I was invited to one of the brothers' birthday party. It was a picnic on a bank of the North Fork of the Canadian River, and the guests were told to dress in costume, with a prize for the winner. Mom sewed some false patches on my overalls, which I wore with a bandanna and beat-up straw hat and some oversized shoes. By a vote of the guests, I won the prize and remember the incident because of my disappointment with it: a silver quarter wrapped in an unused deposit slip from an Okemah bank. What had I expected? Something more, maybe a dollar! After that, a kind of reconciliation took place — or at least the brothers left me alone physically, even though their snobbery persisted. Yet what impressed me most about the older brother was that he wore braces on his teeth. To get them fitted, his mother drove once a month to Oklahoma City. He was the only youngster I knew with braces until I moved to Tulsa, where they still struck me as an oddity even though they seemed rather common there.

The other memorable birthday party I attended in my Okemah days was also given by one of the brothers; it was held in his parents' home in the southern part of town where the best homes were located. The large stucco house had a cavernous dining room, where the feted brother opened his presents and we feasted on ice cream and cake. His mother was a pretty lady, one of the few I knew in Okemah with bobbed hair — and I think she was probably one of the first women I ever saw smoking a cigarette!

After the presents had been opened, we boys went in a group to the Jewel to see the latest motion picture starring Marion Davies; it was a musical, *Singing in the Rain,* and a style new to me. I liked the beautiful Davies and all the singing more than I cared to admit, for I often bragged that only cowboy movies interested me, and more to the point, cowboy pictures that had no girls or romance. But I liked that movie so much I hurried home to tell Mom the plot and describe its lovely star. I could be frank with Mom, but with my friends the conversation turned quickly to Tom Mix or Ken Maynard.

My early schooling exposed me to my first schoolboy crush, for we had a pretty young teacher who was interested in our learning skills as much as our deportment. Owing to her encouragement, I showed an advanced ability to read that soon became a part of my daily life. From the age of five, I raced through the children's books available at the kindergarten. At six I started reading the funny papers, developing an appetite for the likes of "Freckles and His Friends," "Andy Gump," "Alley Oop," and "Out Our Way." This led me into reading the whole newspaper, the *Okemah Daily Leader,* from that time forward. The next step was to obtain a library card, which introduced me to the world of books and allowed me to start checking out all kinds of treasures. Fortunately, the lady in charge of Okemah's public library, then housed in a converted store on Broadway, was not like the one Eudora Welty encountered in her childhood — the Okemah librarian *wanted* us to check out books.

Books for boys in those days were often shelved in series, and my favorite was the redoubtable Tom Swift, the Ivy League hero who could solve all mysteries and overcome all obstacles. *Tom Swift and His Electric Submarine* had my full attention, as did all his various adventures. Then, like Miss Welty, I graduated from potboilers to find that stories about real people were more fun. Histories of pioneers, Indians, soldiers, and warfare began to fill my day.

The day of the dime novel was over, but a substitute was the ten-cent pulp magazines that filled the magazine racks at the local drug stores. Printed on cheap paper, these magazines featured fiction about ace pilots in World War I, cowboy tales, and detective stories that required no thought process whatever. I soon grew tired of them and switched to the Big Little Books popular for a year or so — also printed on cheap paper but about three inches thick and three inches square. They were devoted mainly to such comic characters as Dick Tracy and Little Orphan Annie, and could be read in half an hour, then stored away or swapped to a pal for a different one. This fad disappeared almost as suddenly as it was spawned, so I went back to the city library for more challenging books, i.e., books that had to be taken home and read over the course of a week.

Comic books became popular but not with me. Perhaps it was psychological, for once on the school playground I was permitted to peek at a spurious "Maggie and Jiggs" cartoon, based on a popular comic strip, that was so prurient I was embarrassed and ashamed. One glance was enough for me, which caused the book's owner to label me a "goody-goody" who would not be shown such treasures again. He then showed it to a crowd of older boys eager to learn more about the world of sex beyond Okemah's limits.

From my earliest memory I was always interested in history books. The teacher who encouraged me to read history, Emma Sutherland, assigned me a report on George Washington during a week in February devoted to cutting out silhouettes of the great man and pasting them on our classroom windows, alongside cutouts of cherries and hatchets. (We didn't know or care that Parson Weems's story was part of the Washington mythology). She praised my report and said that I had a natural bent for history. Her attention helped shape my life, for I continued to read the histories and biographies she suggested might interest me. In arithmetic and spelling I was barely able to struggle by, but soon my knowledge of history was expanding and I was reading books beyond those written for a boy my age.

❧

Two incidents related to school stand out. In 1932, a group of Okemah ladies decided to bring culture to town in the form of a traveling art exhibit. they rented poster-sized copies of great masterpieces from leading museums and displayed them for a week in an empty store on Broadway.

To enliven the scene, they asked teachers to choose pupils who could give a short talk as visitors moved about the collection. When our class learned of the event, I decided to use my reading to give me a chance as a guide, for I craved attention. Perhaps that was because I was too short to gain recognition in playground sports, although I tried baseball and football to avoid being called a "sissy." If I could not excel in athletics, what was left? Books, and the pleasure that came from reading them. As the art show would prove, even though Okemah had many drawbacks in the 1930s, it also had some excellent, hard-working teachers, in spite of low pay. Their constant encouragement opened a different world for me.

The picture that attracted me was Sir Joshua Reynolds's *Blue Boy.* I learned everything a boy of ten could learn about the artist and his subject, rehearsed my talk, and waited for auditions. When I spoke about *Blue Boy,* before the whole class, I realized my enthusiasm was being wasted, but during recess, Miss Sutherland called me aside and said I would be one of the guides at the art exhibit. This was the first recognition I'd ever received for something I created (except for the radio joke), and nothing that has come my way since has equaled the thrill I felt when that blessed teacher told me the good news. Even though I enjoyed my day as a guide to Okemah's society ladies, my budding career as a docent was cut short when no more art shows took place.

At that time the grade school, junior high, and high schools all were located on the hilltop on South Third Street. A three-block walk for me, it was uphill in the morning and downhill in the afternoon. The long slope left its mark on me through life because I broke off a front tooth when "belly-whopping" on a sled one a cold February day. Across from the schools there was a low, clapboard candy store where too many of us ventured after school, pennies in hand, for a twisted stick of black licorice or an all-day sucker, which lasted about five minutes. Red "Indian Chief" tablets sold for a five-cent piece, pencils were two for a nickel, and erasers a penny.

When feeling brash, some of us boys would take a piece of candy to the school, hiding it in the desks where books and tablets were kept. This was a minor amusement that, if discovered, at worst only brought down a strong wooden ruler on the offender's outstretched palm. No back-talk was allowed, and rarely was any boy sent to the principal's office for a real shellacking.

The cruelest incident I witnessed in grade school concerned two farm girls who were older than the rest of us, probably twelve or thirteen, and larger and more shapely than the other girls in our class. Perhaps they were kept behind because of their slow aptitudes in reading and writing. They were constant companions at recess and always ate their brown-bag lunches together.

Our teacher insisted that students listen to her in complete silence. To whisper during her soliloquies was to invite her wrath. She could hear the faintest whispering with her radar-like antennae and would immediately call the offender to come forward for a ruler whack. But on this day she spied the two girls trading notes — another taboo in her classes.

"What are you girls doing, passing notes?"

"No, ma'am. That wasn't us."

"Don't lie to me, I saw it. Hand it over!" She stormed to the back of the room, where the older girls sat next to each other.

"Hand it over!" She was reddening, as were the girls. One of them began to cry, then timidly held out her hand with a scrap of paper in it.

The teacher scanned the note as the girls implored her not to read it aloud. Now *she* looked embarrassed. The rest of the class sat silently as the tension made everyone feel uncomfortable. It seemed that even she realized she was going too far, unfairly interfering in their lives.

What the note said remains a mystery to this day, but wild guesses as to the contents flew at recess. Many rumors that night said the note concerned a man one of the girls knew. What the teacher did with the note is also a mystery. The only real fact known is that the two girls dropped out of school a short time later, and I never saw them again. The school grapevine reported not long afterward, however, that one of the girls had married.

I witnessed another case of heartbreak on St. Valentine's Day in the fourth grade. As February 14 approached, we all bought penny valentines at Harkey's 5 & 10 and sent one to the teacher and a few to our buddies, as well as one to another pupil whose name we drew from a box containing a slip for everyone in the class. That way, no one was neglected. But this year, a bright-looking little guy named Jesse Miracle proved to be overly generous. He bought a valentine for everyone and with some pomp placed them in the pile at the front of the room.

When the teacher passed out the valentines, it soon became obvious that Jesse was going to receive at best only one or two. Despite her efforts to explain and to console him, Jesse was so disappointed he began to cry, and as he did, all of us began to regret we hadn't sent Jesse a valentine, too. Jesse recovered and, in time, he became a lawyer and then a judge. I always wondered if he remembered that day when his heart seemed broken.

❧❧ 6 ❧❧

More Joys of Learning

Looking back at the Okemah schools, I believe I was taught by some superior men and women, whose salary was perhaps a hundred dollars a month and for which they worked long hours. I don't recall that we had a parent-teacher association, but we did have dedicated teachers and some school administrators who understood the workings of children's minds.

One educator in the Okemah system believed in incentives, which took the form of exemptions from final tests in a particular course. The exempt pupils were listed a few days before examinations, and one year I was delighted to see my name on the history list. My history teacher was a handsome young man who wielded a heavy paddle, and he once expressed amazement that I could be so feisty and yet do so well in my classwork. To his credit, he did not hold my conduct against me and excused me from his history test. Instead of doing something useful, I spent that free time strutting around the playground, trying to let the world know I was one of the chosen few.

Weekly spelling contest also fostered competition in Okemah's grade school. They were a highlight because we competed for the honor of being the best speller in our room; somehow it was assumed that the pupil who led in spelling was also an overall leader. The teacher would divide the class evenly, then read the words, which we spelled in rotation. When we missed, we sat down and waited, as the tension increased, until finally a winner emerged.

The girls always seemed to win, and we boys would go to recess with sour-grape remarks about how it was "sissy" to win a spelling contest, anyway. But in my heart I loved the chance to show off, to try and prove that a small body with a brain was more valuable than size alone. Not once did I ever win, but I always hoped that someday I might. The value of hope was a lesson learned early in those Okemah classrooms.

We also looked forward to fire drills because a large, steel tunnel running from the second floor to the ground would be opened for the tests. For the firemen, the point was to ring the alarm and time the building's evacuation, but for us the swift slide down the tunnel was great fun and the whole exercise not only disrupting but exciting. Rumors of an impending fire drill kept us on edge, and we managed to stretch a ten-minute routine to thirty minutes before we marched back to our classrooms to resume the day's schedule. Secretly, I sometimes wished for an actual fire, since it would make all those drills worthwhile. What was the point of having them four or five times a year if nothing terrifying ever happened?

The playground between my school and Noble Junior High occasionally became a battlefield, with fistfights over slurs, remarks, petty rivalries, or disputes from a game of "keepers." I had my share of these, including one where a bully promised a feisty little guy a nickel if he could bloody my nose. He accomplished his mission in short order, but in defending myself I tore a finger on the sharp pin holding up his overall straps. With blood flowing, I screamed and ran for home, my own overalls so bloody that it looked like my death was imminent.

The playground also held its share of mysteries. I often found pieces of seashells in the clay dust and I finally took a specimen home to inquire about its origin. "How could a piece of seashell wind up on a hill in Okemah?" I asked Mom in genuine bewilderment.

Her answer bespoke her fundamentalism. "When the earth was flooded and Noah took all his animals into the Ark," she replied matter-of-factly, "God covered the earth with an ocean. When the flooding ended, the whole world was just one big seabed."

That was pretty impressive stuff for a nine-year-old boy. I wanted to know more about Noah and made a point to ask my Sunday school teacher for more explicit information. She came back with a full biblical description of the great flood, with all the animals entering the Ark two by two. This vision was reinforced by a movie depicting the flood I saw about the same time. The story of the Ark became my favorite, and I was quick to point out to companions on the playground the real reason why we had seashells under our feet. Nobody wanted to argue the point.

❁

On the rare occasion, when she had a few extra dollars, Mom would pack me into the Chevrolet and drive to Okmulgee, where she proceeded to the beauty shop for a permanent wave. The thirty-two-mile trip to Okmulgee was punctuated with much conversation, for she often picked up young hitchhikers who liked to tell their life story, perhaps out of gratitude or maybe because the silence was oppressive when three were packed into the single seat. Another diversion, as I learned to read, was to display my newfound skill by reading road signs aloud. My favorites were the Burma Shave advertisements that were posted in sequence, with several words that formed a jingle on each of five or six signs. The signs were nailed to the top of barbed-wire fence posts, and the most memorable was:

Hinky dinky
Parlez-vous
Cheer up the face
The war is through
Burma Shave

That sign took on meaning when Mom explained that American doughboys in France had a favorite song during the world war called "Hinky-dinky parlez-vous." Soon I was watching for all Burma Shave signs, for I was eager to impress our hitchhiking guests with my reading skill.

Our first such trip to Okmulgee scared me, however. Mom took me into a beauty shop that had an ominous look. I was frightened by the clutter, and when I saw the drying machines that fitted over ladies' heads, somehow I concluded that Mom was going to be beheaded. I cried until she took me to the store where my mother worked; such visits were rare because socializing on company time was not allowed. My mother's assurance that nothing untoward would happen in the beauty shop was all I needed to hear, for I took all her words as absolute truth. She consoled and gave me a buffalo-head nickel to spend while my stepgrandmother was being beautified.

Okmulgee was a big city to my young eyes. I liked the sandstone Creek Council House in the town square, and even more to my taste were the five-and-ten stores, which were larger than those in Okemah and stocked with more of my favorite toys, particularly lead soldiers. A Golden Goose hamburger shop emitted enticing, delicious odors, and for dime I feasted on a hamburger and root beer.

Okmulgee had more movie houses than Okemah, but usually we went there on other business. Once, Mom splurged and we drove over to see *Ben Hur,* which had a chariot-racing scene that impressed me mightily; the hero was Ramon Navarro, Mom's favorite motion-picture actor. We visited Okmulgee not long after the Hippodrome Theater burned, leaving a hulk of twisted, steel roofing beams that soon became a classic eyesore. Could this happen to the Crystal or Jewel? I hoped not, since going to the movies was an integral part of Mom's and my life.

As the era of silent movies was ending, Mom was becoming a film addict. When I was still a toddler, she would buy one ticket, settle into the darkened theater with me on her lap, and whisper the captions to keep me abreast of the plot until I fell asleep. When the film ended, she would awaken me and we would trudge back home. If I had become surly after the picture show, Mom would rock me to sleep in front of a gas-jet stove that warmed her chilly bedroom.

When the first talkie was made, a tearjerker titled *The Jazz Singer* starring Al Jolson, Mom was pretty excited about it and wished Okemah had a theater that could show it. Neither theater was equipped for sound at that time. One sunny afternoon, however, rambling up by the Crystal, I saw a large wooden crate by the back entry and assumed it was the long-awaited sound machine that would open the door to talking pictures in our home-town. Without bothering to check the facts with the Crystal's owner, I rushed home to tell Mom that *The Jazz Singer* would soon be playing in Okemah. She was crestfallen that night when Mr. Burke told her the crate contained only a brand-new sign for the theater.

Eventually, sound arrived and the Jolson movie did come to the Crystal; we were there on opening night. The movie was so successful that soon merchandise related to it began to appear. Mom always bought me a new article of clothing to be worn on Easter Sunday, and that year she found a boy's cap in Okmulgee with "Sonny Boy" sewn across the front. This meant a lot to me, for *The Jazz Singer* story involved a youngster who was supposed to be Jolson's son, and I saw myself vicariously as Mom's own sonny boy. I wore the cap to church on Easter and had my picture taken in it at a three-for-a-dime photo booth in an Okmulgee cigar store.

Okmulgee was New York and San Francisco rolled into one during these boyhood years. Across from the Stewart-Luckey Department Store in Okmulgee was a popcorn wagon with a motor-driven popper, which I watched with fascination as a tiny metal clown seemed to be making the popper revolve. Between the popcorn stand and the Golden Goose a block away, the waft of that fragrant mixture of hamburgers and popcorn became part of the Okmulgee scene for me. There was also a kind of ritual in driving past the building where my father had worked until a week before his death. The structure (which was still standing in 1992), had art-deco depictions of winged automobile tires spaced as cornices above the storefront. There my father had sold batteries, rung the cash register, and answered the telephone when my mother called. Somehow I was baffled by the contradiction of a life gone but a building still standing. Or so I thought in my tenth year.

❧ 7 ❧

The Broadway Hotel

My final years in Okemah were spent in a hotel that has long since been torn down. At the time of the oil boom, between 1919 and 1924, it had been a bustling center for land men, pipeline dealers, and wildcatters, but by 1932 it was a deserted eyesore, with a sign in peeling paint: Broadway Hotel.

Mom's unhappiness must have led to her decision to break away from Pop and run a hotel. The domestic crisis behind the move was hidden from me; however, I became aware of a change when she told the boarders she would be closing the Third Street house as soon as she found larger quarters. Mom had a hard time making up her mind, and she did not trust her judgment. She faced two rather depressing choices: a small two-story hotel across from the courthouse, which was offered to her for a low price, and the three-story Broadway Hotel at the corner of First and Broadway, which was empty but needing repair. This was in 1933, when Pop was still blaming Hoover for everything wrong with the country. His electric motor had burned out, so he closed the mill; maybe that's why Mom decided to pull up stakes. The pipeline crews had disappeared, filling stations were going out of business, and corn and cotton prices had plunged.

Whatever her reasons, Mom and I drove over to Ada to ask a black fortune-teller for help in deciding which hotel to buy. This was an old habit of hers; more than once we had driven to nearby Castle for a consultation with a palm-reader. An acquaintance of Mom's reported that the fortune-teller in Ada was a marvel at foreseeing the future, and even though Ada was thirty miles away, Mom wanted the best possible advice. The fortune-teller in Ada took her two dollars and told Mom what she wanted to hear.

A few days later she took me to Tulsa, where she met with an official of the Atlas Life Insurance Company, owners of the decrepit building. A deal was struck that allowed her to use the building without paying any rent, the point being that an empty building would soon become worthless. Plumbing, painting, and plaster repairs would be Mom's responsibility, and if she succeeded, they would talk about leases later.

Within a few weeks she had cleaned up the ground and first floors, scrubbed the kitchen, and had tables and chairs built from pine boards, then stained and varnished. The lobby walls were painted, the stairs given a new coat of varnish, and a pay telephone booth placed in one corner of the enormous room. Across the lobby window a freshly painted red-and-silver sign proclaimed: Broadway Hotel. Several large ferns were located strategically to make the lobby look more attractive, and the sofa from our Third Street house was placed next to the brass spittoon Mom bought to accommodate the tobacco-chewers.

Later that summer of 1933, a big poster was placed in the front window, a red, white, and blue display with a huge eagle in the middle over the initials "N.R.A." I was told it had something to do with President Roosevelt but didn't mean much, which proved to be the case. There were no pictures on the lobby walls, only a bank calendar.

Mom brought every stick of furniture from the Third Street house to fill up the hotel rooms and moved the gas

stove that had served at the boardinghouse into the cavernous kitchen. She had storage bins built with hinged doors
to protect food from the rats rumored to reside in the vicinity, and set up a makeshift table in the dining hall, between
the lobby and kitchen.

Pop did not fit into Mom's new plans. He was left at
the mill, living in the lean-to room that had once been used
by Ben. I did not like the smell of the place and was sorry
Pop didn't move with us. He assured me we would see
each other every day, but I soon learned that would be possible only if I went by the mill on my way home from
school. My grandfather and his wife had become strangers,
and rather bitter ones, but I was only vaguely aware of this
tense domestic tragedy.

The change of scenery gave Mom a new vitality. She
was too fond of her own cooking and had become overweight, but the work required to make the hotel usable had
caused her to slim down. To contribute to the new image,
she sent me to the drugstore to buy a can of henna, and her
hair became redder as her cheeks became more rosy.

❀

After our move to Mom's rejuvenated Broadway
Hotel, from that time forward I saw less of Pop. When we
left, he moved into the front bedroom at the old house but
later went to Shawnee. In addition to her beds from the
boardinghouse, Mom bought some secondhand ones and
also some ancient dressers and rugs, and started a new life
as the owner-manager-cook of the establishment.

The Broadway Hotel was on the right side of the
tracks, geographically, but on the wrong side socially, a fact
I learned that fall when my birthday loomed. Mom told me
I could invite four friends and promised to bake a cake and

pay our way to the movies. The Jewel Theater was in our block and was the social center of that end of town, so I was anxious to see what movie would be shown there on the weekend. Saturday movies featured the likes of Buck Jones, Bob Steele, Ken Maynard, Tim McCoy, and my favorite — the taciturn Tom Mix. Before the cowboy picture there was an Our Gang comedy or a Laurel and Hardy two-reeler, plus the serials that always ended with the hero about to fall over a cliff or face a similar ghastly fate.

As it turned out, which movie had been scheduled was not important, because only one of the three boys I invited came to my party. I later learned that the mothers of the other two would not let them go to "that hotel." To a tousle-headed L. D. Tindall, who did come, I was committed to a friendship forever. Gradually it dawned on me that the many comings and goings of couples without luggage through the hotel lobby gave the place a reputation among the standard setters of Okemah society. The night clerk explained that the couples with no luggage paid in advance because they were gone by midnight.

Children are slow to perceive situations, but once they do, it's with a sharp focus. After the disappointing birthday I began to notice the two ladies Mom had taken on as boarders; both were young, and both had male visitors on the weekends. One was a rather washed-out woman with a boy so young we couldn't be playmates. Her rent, I found out, was paid each Saturday by the owner of a local auto supply business. He came and went, sometimes at lunchtime, sometimes on Saturdays and Sundays.

The other woman was only a girl, about nineteen or twenty, pretty, frightened, and pregnant. Slowly the truth behind her presence at the hotel sank in, for she was visited on weekends by a man in his fifties who owned a Henryetta picture show. The girl had been his employee in the box office. She stayed in her room most of the time but seemed to like to talk with me about movies we had seen or hoped to see. As she grew bigger, she became more frightened. Then one day her room was empty, and I was sorry to hear she had been taken to a hospital to have her baby. There is no sequel, except that Mom warned me, when we occasionally went to Henryetta, never to mention the girl's name. Another secret! This hidden knowledge was burdensome because the bus station in Henryetta was also a drugstore and a font of information to the community. The bus from Okemah to Tulsa stopped there for passengers and rest rooms, and whenever I passed through, I was tempted to ask the young man behind the soda fountain what had become of my favorite boarder. But I never did.

❖

The move to the Broadway Hotel was the beginning of the end of my stay in Okemah. Even though I had grown accustomed to the routine of my life there, I sometimes despaired that my prayers to join my mother would ever be answered. When she visited on occasional Sundays, she saw that living conditions were not ideal for an eleven-year-old boy. The depression was grinding everyone over twenty-one down a notch or two, but children were not affected so much as long as they ate well — which we did because Mom and her helpers ran the hotel like a boarding-house early on, offering both board and room for six dollars a week. Our clothes were worn but clean, the car was a few years' old but still running, and Mom's credit at Mr. Meredith's grocery store was good. In small-town America, the standard breakfast was bacon and eggs, biscuits, and coffee; lunch was usually a slice of meat loaf or pork chop served with huge helpings of green beans and canned tomatoes, and a pudding dessert. For supper there would be roasts, pork chops, or stews, with cobblers or pies for dessert. Mom settled with the Merediths and other merchants at the end of each month.

The trouble was, after all the settling, nothing of consequence would be left. This was the painful conclusion I reached in the summer of 1933, when my mother invited me to come to Tulsa to see the circus. The Al G. Barnes circus, featuring the cowboy movie star Tim McCoy, was coming to Tulsa, and I had hinted to her in a postcard that I would sure like to see that famous man. The bus fare for a youngster on the red-and-cream Union Transportation Company bus was half the adult cost, or eighty-five cents. I showed my mother's letter to Mom, and she looked a bit wary. She kept all her cash in a china jar, and at this time it held a single dollar bill.

This crisis brought the depression home to me. But Mom did not hesitate; she handed me the dollar and assured me that someone who owed money on his board bill would be paying in a day or two. Despite a twinge of conscience, I took the dollar and packed my things in a cheap cardboard valise. Through some mixup, my mother was not at the Tulsa bus station to meet me, and I lost my only nickel when trying to call her at the roominghouse where she lived, near the Swan Lake area in Tulsa. So I walked from the bus station to her house, following the bus route I already knew, entered her empty room, and went to bed without any supper. The excitement about the circus was the only nourishment I needed, and my stepgrandmother's sacrifice was partially justified by the thrill of a seeing Tim McCoy sweep past my seat the next night.

Money seemed to be a constant problem from 1933 on. There was an excellent bakery in Okemah run by the Cox brothers, and I had often stopped there and charged a pie to Mom's account. But in the summer of 1933, I charged an apricot pie, and took it to the Broadway, whereupon she gave me a good scolding. She hardly ever raised her voice to me, so I understood I had frivolously spent twenty-five cents and should not do it again.

The loss of a half a dollar was a near tragedy, as I learned when a counterfeit fifty-cent piece came into the hotel till; it was not discovered until the next day, when the once-shiny coin had turned a dull gray and made a clanking sound when dropped in with the real silver. Mom had bought some hair-coloring known as Egyptian Henna for ten cents at a bankruptcy sale in Okmulgee, which she now had me take to the druggist up the street and ask him for a refund *without a receipt*. I did as I was told, and although the druggist seemed upset, he gave me eighty-five cents in change. Mom hugged me when I brought her the profits from this questionable scheme; I was of two minds, for I knew we needed the extra seventy-five cents. But it was acquired with some sense of guilt.

More honorable was the time Mom cashed in a five-dollar gold piece my mother had given her for a Christmas present, which the government now ordered redeemed for cash, even though the law allowed collectors to save their gold. Because that five dollars meant so much to Mom, we promised each other not to tell my mother how her present had been turned into hard cash.

Even more poignant was the price battle that developed between the Hotel and the rival boardinghouse across the street. Mom had a large sign painted and erected on the corner of First and Broadway offering a week's board and room for the cut rate of $5.50. Next day, the rival had a smaller sign offering the same for $5. Mom responded with a hand-painted alteration of her sign, cutting her price to $4.50. That was her last desperate gesture, and the price dropped no further below this pitiful figure. Meager as this seems, remember that a dozen eggs cost only fifteen cents, milk was a nickel a quart, and other foods sold proportionately.

With money a constant topic of conversation, I was alert for opportunities to make more in addition to bottle deposits or scrap metal sales. When a building on lower Broadway was torn down, and the construction boss announced his company would pay workers who cleaned and stacked the bricks. I borrowed a hatchet from Pop and started making my own pile, then enlisted other boys who agreed to add to my stack on the theory that small stacks would be stolen when one's back was turned. Since it was summertime, this was hot work and required a good many trips to the hotel for ice water for my crew; I spent most of my time relaying water to the workers who cleaned bricks or trying to prevent the silent transfer of bricks from one pile to another..

The job took a couple of weeks, and some of the unemployed men competing with my crew resented the presence of children. This competition proved to be short-lived, however, when the first piles of bricks were "bought back" from the hatchet-wielders for pitifully low prices. The word spread, and yet I persisted in the hope that my managerial skill would bring me as much as a dollar profit in the final settlement.

When all the bricks were cleaned and the boss assessed each pile's value, I found that after paying off the other boys I emerged with a profit of fifteen cents. I reported this disappointment to Mom, but she only laughed and explained that a vague contract was no contract, and I should take the experience as a lesson in dealing with strangers.

One stranger who was a hotel tenant for a while made a living trading newspaper subscriptions for chickens. He drove a Model A Ford that had several tiers of chicken coops mounted in place of a missing rumble seat. He left the hotel early each morning and returned at night with the coops full of hens, along with a few crates of eggs, some butter, and a variety of farm produce. He made a commission by selling his traded goods, then paying for the subscriptions and pocketing the remaining cash. It was not a good way to make a living, I decided, when he told Mom that the weekly returns on his swapping left him with only a few dollars, once he paid his gasoline bill.

More profitable was the store next door, which was part of the hotel building. It stood empty for months until a promoter rented it from Mom to exhibit an automobile full of bullet holes, said to have been the car in which some desperado, perhaps Matt Kimes, was killed. Kimes was a local folk hero, as was "Pretty-Boy" Floyd, a small-time criminal still alive in 1933. His reputation in Oklahoma was more that of a Robin Hood; he had come from the Kiamichi Mountain region of southeastern Oklahoma and "only" robbed such fair game as banks. The exhibit also contained wax models of Kimes and several other notorious bank robbers, but business was so slow that a projected long-term engagement ended after a few days.

The next potential tenant was a blonde-haired businessman who wanted to establish a kind of pawnshop in the empty store, to be called "Dynamite Mac's," where used clothing and other secondhand merchandise would be sold. He also planned to buy watches, jewelry, gold, and silver, and would have his store manager pay for both board and room at the hotel. Actual cash payments for rent would begin once the store succeeded.

Mom agreed to the enterprise, and the secondhand shop was soon in business. The man left in charge wore striped shirts and talked a lot at mealtimes. He foresaw a chain of successful secondhand stores across Oklahoma because nothing in the store sold for more than a few dollars. He was full of advice on how to save money. Used clothing was a good buy, he ventured, because most suits and coats could be rejuvenated with dry cleaning. Thus, for two dollars, a man might have a suit made by Hart, Shaffner & Marx that was hardly worn at the elbows. Shoes, however, were another matter.

"Never buy used shoes," he warned. "They already have the contours of somebody else's feet and have fungus that carries athlete's foot or something like it."

I did not know what "athlete's foot" was, but it was a lesson in bargain hunting that I remembered.

The new store seemed to prosper, and I tried to talk Pop into visiting it. The place was full of great buys, including some secondhand shotguns and I knew Pop liked to go hunting and had once been a good shot. He was not interested, however. In fact, Pop rarely came to the Broadway Hotel — probably to avoid confronting Mom's live-in friend — and my only memory of his visiting was that he came with a BB gun and took a post by the swinging door into the kitchen in late afternoon to shoot the sewer rats that emerged when the kitchen lights were turned off; the rats became so destructive she allowed Pop to come with his air rifle. He had not lost his ability to aim precisely, with the help of some "dime-store" spectacles, and he was discreet in disposing of his victims. Although the food was stored in wooden cabinets with stout doors, occasional scraps on the floor attracted the rodents. Mom warned me not to go in the kitchen after dark, and I was under a bond of silence, whenever boarders raved about the good flavor and quantity of food Mom provided, never to mention the rat problem.

❀

Mom's life changed considerably when two insurance men from Texas appeared at the hotel one day and took a room for a two-week stay. At the end of the first week, the older salesman moved in with Mom and after that I slept on a pallet at the end of foot bed. I made the situation into an adventure by pretending I was camping out in the woods, and except for the mice scurrying around the floor at night, it was not bothersome.

But in the town of Okemah it was not long before there was talk, which meant that eventually trouble would appear. It came one summer afternoon when I saw Mom's new friend walking into the lobby with a torn shirt and blood on his face. I sympathized and followed him to Mom's room, where she began to cry and sob convulsively as she wiped away the blood. He had gone to the filling station for gas, and the attendant had made a crude remark about a man who would live with another man's wife "in broad daylight." A fistfight followed, and a report of the incident swept through the lower Broadway section. My prayers to move to Tulsa probably intensified that night.

❧❧ 8 ❧❧

Movies and Other Important Pastimes

The fistfight and dark mutterings I overheard worried me. I was not able to understand where my grandfather fitted into the picture, and Mom was more on edge after the filling station incident. Still, much went on to make life good. Thursday night was Buddy Night at the Jewel, with a sack of popcorn thrown in if I had a spare nickel. After we moved to the hotel, Mom had more boarders who liked movies, so I could make an arrangement to go in advance and not have to pester lonesome strangers.

The radio in our bedroom was not used much; but once when I had the measles, I listened to it throughout the day and first heard a memorable song, "Smoke Gets in Your Eyes," which I thought was extra good. Mom and her friend did not listen to "Amos n' Andy" or anything I can recall except the Lightcrust Doughboys, who played on a Dallas station we could get without static. Mom's Texan friend liked to hear the program's announcer, W. Lee O'Daniel, who sold flour and spoke in low-key homilies that seemed to have a moral point most of the time. Sometimes I also listened to an afternoon serial, "Little Orphan Annie," but not often, because as it took time away from football and baseball games played near the ice plant. Reading and movies were my favored forms of entertainment.

Saturday mornings were special because for a dime the Jewel offered a serial, a cowboy movie, and a cartoon or comedy. Bill Slepka, the manager, also experimented with pie-eating contests, amateur talent shows, and other promotions for his young audiences. After one dismal effort at pie-eating, with chocolate smeared over my face and hair, I decided I had no theatrical talent: let others take the stage.

The big promotion that excited Okemah was provided by a stranger who came to town, made a contract with the Crystal Theater and began to advertise in the *Leader* that Elmer's Big Country Store would offer hundreds of prizes two weeks hence. The top awards were a one-hundred dollar discount on a Ford and a fifty-dollar discount on a Zenith radio. These were hefty savings because that same week, Barry's Chevrolet Agency was advertising a comparable a six-cylinder standard model for $445. Merchants gave tickets in return for purchases, from which the winning numbers would be drawn.

Elmer's store provided my introduction to big-time corruption. I happened to be in Mom's room when the promoter "Elmer" asked her and her live-in friend if they would be interested in winning the larger discount. With scarcely five dollars to her name, Mom said yes, and in short order the promoter made a deal. He would take the number of one of her tickets and call it out on the final night. In return, she would not charge him for his two weeks' room and board.

Whatever misgivings I had about this crooked deal were compounded the last night. I had collected fifty or sixty of the numbered tickets and was seated on the front row of the Crystal as the raffle began. First, the promoter gave away baskets of groceries, then certificates for flowers, shoes, or oil changes. The momentum built up in the full theater when it came time to award the certificate for the radio. He dipped into the basket and pulled one of my numbers; because I knew of the crooked deal about to unfold, I almost kept silent. But in the end, greed took command. I strutted onto the stage and claimed the fifty-dollar prize. Then the promoter surreptitiously read Mom's ticket number off of his shirt cuff (I had seen him write it there back at the hotel), and her live-in friend claimed the one-hundred dollar award. I was afraid someone might protest on the spot, for the two top prizes went to the same household. But Mom's friend was not well known, and I guess that saved us from public suspicion.

The story continued, however, for the local junk dealer came to the hotel a few days later. I assumed he wanted to see Mom, but no, he wanted to see me. My grandfather had bought a used automobile engine from him to replace a burned-out one but had never paid for it. The junk dealer offered to forget Pop's bill if I would surrender the radio discount letter in exchange. I felt good about this, for it relieved Pop at a time when his morale was so low. Mom and her friend had less luck. When she told the Ford salesman they were interested in buying a new car, he was elated momentarily, until he saw the discount letter and his ardor drooped. Neither Mom nor the Texan had money for a car at any price, so the time limit expired with the corrupted letter still in Mom's dresser drawer.

There was one more story related to the big giveaway. While it was being advertised in the *Leader*, I had wandered into one of the five-and-ten stores and become intrigued with a toy catalog resting on a counter. The booklet was full of delights but none was more alluring than a red coaster wagon with "pants" (in imitation of covered wheels on airplanes) over its four wheels. It cost about four dollars, and I wondered aloud if it could be ordered. Carl Meador, the clerk, assured me it could. I raced home and painted a vision of this lovely wagon for Mom, stating my willingness to wait until Christmas for such a gift, but she interrupted to say, "If you win a big prize in the lottery at the Crystal, I'll get the wagon for you before Christmas." At the time, no doubt, she meant only to give me something to hope for, but my spirits soared with her promise. With a child's lack of knowledge, or an effort to ignore the reality of our finances, I was ready to claim my prize when I won the radio discount.

How much of a sacrifice my greediness entailed for Mom she kept from me. About a month after the lottery, my red superwagon arrived at the store and was on display when I made my daily visit of inquiry. Like the Stutz Bearcat, the wagon was my dream come true; Mom kept her promise and bought it for me. Every night I carefully parked it on the hotel's covered porch, because some of my toys had been disappearing in the vicinity. Eventually, my beautiful wagon also vanished, and although I felt the loss, something pretty important had come with the wagon, which gave me a feeling of great respect for Mom. A grown-up had kept her word.

Since my playmates and I had little hard cash, we improvised cops-and-robbers games using ten-cent cap pistols or homemade wooden guns that shot "bullets" made from cut-up inner tubes. Even direct hits barely stung, as we pretended to be infamous desperadoes or Tim Mix, if the game was cowboys and Indians. Treeclimbing was important, too, as were roller-skating, sandlot baseball, and touch football games. On rainy or blustery days Mom often had a jigsaw puzzle laid out on the dining room table, and a five-hundred-piece puzzle costing a quarter could occupy several days before the last piece (if not lost) was inserted in mock triumph.

My favorite pastime was playing war games with lead soldiers. Most of the soldiers were infantrymen who withstood a barrage of small pebbles until al the arms and legs were broken off. I knew just enough history to have a favorite, a mounted "General Pershing" who wore a World War I tin helmet over a grim visage. Even when his horse had lost its legs and his painted face was pockmarked with scars, I sent him into daily battle until finally the general's head was knocked off in mortal combat. I buried him in the backyard with full honors.

Springtime was marble season. Although I was a poor shot in marble games, I had two prize agates my mother had brought me on a Sunday visit. I was afraid to risk them in a game, so I kept them wrapped in a piece of paper, apart from my regular doogies. For some reason I brought the wrapped agates down to the lobby one evening to show them off to some of the clientele, and when my bragging time was over, I left them on a table beside a potted fern.

On the following morning the wrapping was there but the agates were not. Instead of looking on the floor to see if they had worked loose and rolled off, I assumed a thief had been at work during the night and ran to the courthouse to report my loss to a deputy sheriff. His name was Bob Taylor, and he was the friendly deputy we all knew because he wore a pearl-handled pistol in his holster. Mr. Taylor, whose main job seemed to be walking up and down Broadway late in the evening, checking to see if doors had been duly locked, listened to my story sympathetically; he urged me to make a careful search before I went to the trouble of filing an "official" report. The agates were probably lost through carelessness and laziness, because the idea of making my little molehill into a mountain was more than I was prepared to do.

9

Small-Town Diversions

Indians were all around me in Okemah, but I had no reason to think of them as any different from my other schoolmates. It was a color-blind society in one respect and terribly bigoted in another. The Indian men in the wagon yard on Saturday night were no better or worse than the white men who caroused on lower Broadway and picked fights outside the pool hall. The Indians who were my heroes were named Harjo and Tiger; the best athletes on the Okemah High School football and basketball teams came from large Creek families that bore those names.

Football games were played on the baseball diamond on the western edge of town, because a fence surrounded the ballpark. In the fall it was marked off into a football field, and the Okemah "Panthers" always featured one or more Tigers or Harjos. The equipment was fairly simple — helmets and shoulder pads, duck pants and shoes with cleats. If two hundred people came to a game against Weleetka or Prague, it was a big turnout. There was no effort to establish a state championship; the game was still for students. Indian athletes dominated the running game in football, and a player named Tiger or Harjo had to be taken seriously.

Because Okemah High School had no gym, its home basketball games were played in makeshift auditoriums. One site was an empty warehouse behind the Broadway

Hotel, where a hardwood floor was put down and rickety bleacher seats erected. Small boys could always manage to sneak into these games without paying the twenty-five-cent admission fee. The building had no showers, so in the winter when the heat was on and the going hot-and-heavy, the place had a locker-room aroma. Nobody objected in those days because deodorants were only for sissies, an oft-used and highly pejorative term in Okemah.

The scores in basketball games were low. Okemah might defeat Wetumka eighteen to twelve, and then lose the next game to Paden, fifteen to ten. Indians did not excel in basketball as in football, and since blacks were not allowed to go to white schools, Negro athletes were nonexistent at the games.

All young boys tried to play baseball; the game whetted their desire to become stars in the big leagues. Although some people listened to the World Series on radio, it was still a shared social experience in Okemah. The series was so important that Broadway was roped off between Third and Fourth Streets and a large signboard was erected in front of Roger Standley's radio shop. The board had a diamond with red, green, and white lights, and an announcer would tell a crowd of perhaps six hundred standing or sitting on the curbs who was at bat, who was pitching, and who was on base. When a batter singled, a light would flash on the diamond, and when a home run was hit, all the lights would flash off and on.

As radio reception improved, the roped-off street and other paraphernalia became unnecessary within a few years. But before that symptom of progress took its toll at World Series time, I looked forward to the excitement probably more than such holidays as the Fourth of July or Halloween. My last World Series in Okemah was the 1933 battle between the New York Giants and the Washington Senators; Broadway had a holiday-like atmosphere with a hamburger stand temporarily erected and sunny weather.

St. Louis was the closest big city to Oklahoma with a major league team; therefore the Cardinals were crowd favorites, and players from Oklahoma were prominent folk heroes. Although he did not play for the Cardinals, my favorite was Carl Hubbell of the New York Giants. Hubbell grew up in Meeker, near Shawnee, and was the epitome of the quiet-spoken athlete who seldom bragged. Hubbell won the first and last game of that 1933 World Series, which made him the pride of Oklahoma for a while.

I knew from reading the newspapers that Hubbell was the Giants' "meal-ticket" because of his dependability. During the winter months, he returned to Oklahoma for quail hunting and a much-deserved rest. Whether he ever received as much as twenty thousand dollars for his marvelous pitching feats is unlikely, and I was saddened to learn in 1988 that Hubbell died an almost forgotten man.

Before radio, the newspapers made great heroes out of the likes of Babe Ruth and Hubbell, and sad to say, the more a player womanized and drank, the more a hero he became in some newspaper columns. But Hubbell kept to himself, stayed married to one woman his entire life, and went quietly into the Cooperstown Hall of Fame, just as he had done during his active pitching career.

We did not like to mix sex and sport in Okemah, and our ideal was a man whose worst vice was chewing tobacco. *All* baseball players chewed tobacco, so that was okay. When I tried to chew some Beechnut brand and became sick, I knew a career in baseball was beyond my reach. I hoped Carl Hubbell didn't chew, but if he did, it would have been all right. Heroes deserve extra privileges, it seems.

❖

A promoter, who stayed at the Broadway Hotel, made a half-hearted attempt to bring boxing to Okemah, but he was not skilled and his boxing cards lost money, so he abandoned the effort. Why pay to watch two men slugging when plenty of action occurred on weekends around the pool hall? And on the schoolground, as I well knew.

My first fight, brought on by the bully who promised another boy a nickel if he could bloody my nose, led to further intimidation by this bully, who apparently saw hilarity in pushing me around on the playground. Then an incident took place in the classroom involving him, and the teacher told the boy he would be staying after school for punishment. The bully looked around at me, with a look I still remember, and shook his fist in my direction, muttering something to the effect that when he was out of "detention," he was going to beat me up. For some reason, I was being detained too.

Two classmates had seen the bullying and knew of the larger boy's threat. One of the boys, who had moved to town only recently, assured me he didn't like bullies in general and this one in particular. His name was "Frenchy."

"I'll walk home with you when you get out of detention," he said. A second friend also was ready to fight my battle and said he was coming too.

Now the battle was joined, and when the bully and I were allowed to leave the school, my friends were waiting. The bully, challenged, said he would lick both of them and then start on me. The fight began, and Frenchy had the better of it. The bully finally fell to the ground and began to cry, and we all walked away, leaving him in a crumpled heap.

My hopes were too high, however, for the threats continued, even though I was never beaten or slapped by that bully again. Not long after my defenders had stopped his threatened beating, however, he became the object of my pity. In the middle of the playground, which served the senior, junior, and elementary schools, was a gazebo-like structure where pupils brought lunches and ate during the noon hour. At this particular lunchtime, another and bigger bully had taken a dislike to the one who made life so miserable for me. He found a piece of pie that had been dropped on the ground and was covered with grass and dirt, and he forced the bane of my existence to eat several bites before he stopped twisting his arm. It was pretty disgusting and proof of what my Sunday school teacher had said. "Fighting is bad and always makes life worse on the one who starts the trouble," she admonished us during a class discussion of some biblical theme. Her words came back to me as I watched my nemesis being mistreated. And, sad to say, nobody tried to make the bigger bully stop.

❀

The Fourth of July was a favorite holiday because it meant lots of cheap firecrackers, torpedoes, skyrockets, roman candles, sparklers, and the thrill of danger to life and limb that went with those menaces. Mom warned me about acquaintances who had died of lockjaw, the dreaded tetanus, as a consequence of having a finger blown off by a firecracker that exploded prematurely. Although I managed to burn a finger or two every Fourth, I was ever mindful of her warning. It helped that I was always too eager to wait until dark to set off skyrockets, starting while it was still daylight and I could see clearly.

Fireworks were sold legally in Okemah from about the first of June onward, so I collected a boxful by almost daily purchases. These included tiny "ladyfingers," small crackers with a clay base that could be separated and fired while held between thumb and forefinger; a cache of larger firecrackers that made a loud noise, and if they misfired, could be cut open and fired as fizzlers; a variety of snakes that bubbled forth in a sulphurous cloud; penny rockets, parachute rockets — my favorite, although they cost twenty-five-cents each, so I could buy only one for my hoard; and aerial bombs that went up into the sky and exploded with a thunderous bang.

An ordinance banned the shooting of fireworks on any day but the Fourth, which was the only curb on using our deadly arsenals. I arose around 7:00 a.m. on that day and would set off a few small firecrackers before breakfast, then join other boys for sham battles until the day wore on and we awaited dusk to start our aerial displays. There was no public display, probably because the town fathers thought it wasteful to spend good money on something so ephemeral as a skyrocket. The last fireworks usedwere the sparklers, which we ignited with sticks of "punk" (longer-burning sparklers) and threw into the air as we fired off pinwheels nailed into tree trunks. That was the grand finale, followed by an ice-cream cone before we headed for bed.

The other memorable Okemah holidays were Armistice Day and Halloween. Halloween held a tinge of autumn coolness in the air, the leaves on locust trees had started dropping, and the merchants on Broadway began covering their storefront windows with glycerine around 4:00 p.m. By dusk we youngsters would rush around with bars of laundry soap, mischievously marking any windows with no protective cover. We also wore costumes, usually made from leftover pieces of yard goods; two that I remember were Indian and cowboy outfits Mom made for me. We would parade up and down Broadway for an hour or so, admiring or disparaging other costumes and trying to recognize who wore papier-mâché masks of demons and devils. A few elegant, older couples came each year dressed as southern belles and gentlemen, and there was much hilarity when someone's identity was discovered.

That was the custom on Broadway. Trick or treating was not practiced, but off on the side streets marauding gangs of teenagers with a destructive bent let the air out of tires, threw toilet paper rolls into trees to make an unsightly mess, and looked on the outdoor toilets that still remained in Okemah as fair game. In 1928 these young devils toppled the outhouse next to my grandfather's mill. Mom said she was glad it happened, as the toilet brought a crowd near the house, which she didn't like, and the stench in summertime was offensive. Pop had the outhouse dismantled and the gaping hole in the ground filled with trash, dirt, and corn cobs; he kept a pile there for users instead of a Montgomery Ward catalog, as my Aunt Ethel did. It gave our backyard a better tone immediately, so I was also grateful to the mischief-makers.

Armistice Day was noisy, because the local National Guard unit staged a sham battle in the city park between Second and Third Streets. The Okemah unit was part of the Forty-Fifth Division, which at the time had a shoulder patch of a red-and-yellow swastika, adopted before Hitler used the Indian sign for the Nazi logo. Dressed in battle regalia, our friends and neighbors wore their wool khaki-colored uniforms, complete with campaign hats and puttees wrapped around their calves, and fired blank shells at each other from Springfield rifles or the .30-caliber machine gun used for training. Along with other boys I trailed behind the machine gun, picking up the expended brass as it spewed; the weapon sounded loud but otherwise was harmless.

On Armistice Day we had a school holiday. A parade took place around noon following the sham battle, which featured the black drum-and-bugle corps from Boley mentioned earlier. Parades were rare events in Okemah, and each one was more exciting to anticipate than the actual spectacle, when it finally took place. The Okemah High School band that marched was outclassed by the swinging band from Boley, and also, if my memory is correct, it could not afford uniforms. The presence of a dozen or so horsemen mounted on cow ponies and seated on expensive, silver-worked saddles, gave the parade more form.

Memorial Day came at the end of May, and preparations for the trip to the cemetery began a week earlier. Mom knew how to make flowers out of tissue paper; the process required cutting out patterns on the paper and punching them onto strands of baling wire that became the stems of our artificial flowers when wrapped in green crepe paper. Mom's parents were buried in the first lot at Highland Cemetery, and her father's grave always had a flag placed on it by the American Legion to honor him as a Civil War veteran. That made an impression on me, as did the many hours spent making both the decorations for those graves and the little bouquet for my father's grave, which I created.

Usually there was a ceremony at Highland that day, with an honor guard from the Legion firing a salute; it made a wonderful sound and left the air hazy with smoke and the pungent smell of gunpowder. Long rows of elm trees lined each of the cemetery sections, and Mom made her customary comment about the good job Mr. Payne was doing to "keep up the place" as we headed down the hill for home.

In my praise of small-town America I must not forget the most obvious irreplaceable institution: the blacksmith shop. There were two in Okemah in the late 1920s, but the one where I chose to hang out was on South First Street, not far from the Broadway Hotel. The blacksmith was a tall man who wore spectacles and a large, drooping black mustache. He kept up a constant clanging going from early morning until the late afternoon, and it was a music that was part of small-town American life from the eighteenth century until the automobile and farm tractor made blacksmiths, as the British say, "redundant."

Although blacksmiths could do a variety of things with a piece of bar iron, their stock-in-trade was shoeing horses and repairing wagons and plows. At least, those are the endeavors he pursued on Saturdays when, keeping my distance, I watched him handle a stubborn mare, then calm a mule and shoe him, or forge a new blade to fit a hay-mower or other farm implement. In summer, the shop temperature must have reached 120 degrees, but he always wore a shirt, a leather apron, and a dirty pair of dungarees.

After the blacksmith forged his horseshoes, he would dip them in a large barrel of water, and the hiss of the red-hot iron plunged into the barrel was a sound I equated with "job well done." Of all the sounds, the clang of the blacksmith's hammer striking the anvil was the most distinctive; from a distance of fifty yards it sounded like a magical tinkling bell. I talked to Pop about the possibility of becoming a blacksmith someday, but he discouraged me from such a career. "A blacksmith has to be tall and strong, for he must make horses and mules do as he wants, and you and I are too little to ever make a horse afraid of us." Pop was about five feet, five inches tall and seemed to think I was set for the same pattern. So I reluctantly abandoned another potential career.

The blacksmith was not a man given to great humor, but he was happy to make rings for us boys out of a horse-shoe nail whenever business was quiet. He made one for me and tossed it over while I was daydreaming, and I ran home to show it to Mom.Then I placed it among my other treasures in a cigar box I kept in the bedroom.

The El Verso wooden cigar box that held my most priceless objects was my special joy. It contained several Indian-head pennies, a nickel dated 1856, and a glass bottle shaped like a pistol Mom's sister from Joplin gave to me when she alighted from the train in Henryetta. It was filled with some pill-like colored candies, but when empty it was even better than my iron pistol that shot caps from red rolls of paper charges.

This lady, whose husband was a brakeman for the Missouri-Pacific Railroad, visited Okemah about once a year. Even though I liked the glass pistol, I was not overly fond of her, because she was always full of advice. She thought the idea of my being a blacksmith was ridiculous but was anxious for me to settle on a profession. "You're never too young to start on a life of work," she said. "So what are you going to do when you grow up?"

After abandoning careers as a fireman and aviator, I was uncertain about where I was headed and said so. But I threw in the thought that I was pretty good at drawing pictures.

"Fine," she said, "maybe you can become something useful such as a sign painter."

Being a sign painter had little appeal to me, but I didn't argue since she was a formidable woman who always wore brown-tinted spectacles and a long black or brown dress, with frizzy hair that stood out like she had just been electrified. Her advice was not confined to me but covered all facets of Mom's life, my grandfather's dissolute existence, and the Okemah community in general. I came to suspect that her husband was glad to see her go to Okemah and sorry to see her come back.

The more I looked around, the more bad marriages I saw. But a ten-year-old is no expert at marriage counseling, and when I was told my mother was "going with" an Okmulgee man she might marry, I prayed that he would be a paragon such as my father had been. If he smoked or drank, I knew she would not be interested. At least, I hoped she wouldn't.

When we went to Henryetta to meet the train bringing Mom's sister from Joplin, we drove through the remains of what was once a booming oil field near Cromwell, Oklahoma. The area became a desolate wasteland when the boom ended; the pumping wells leaked oil into surrounding creeks, killing trees and polluting the running streams. Many years later, when I first saw the landscape around the thermal springs in Yellowstone Park, it reminded me of the dismal scene around Cromwell. We also passed the road to Nuyaka, an Indian settlement north of the highway. I wanted to visit the place because I thought it was New York, with a slovenly pronunciation, and I expected to see skyscrapers there. When I finally explained my curiosity to Mom, she smiled and assured me there were no tall buildings in Nuyaka, which was only a wide place in the road. It was a Creek town named after a village left behind "back East" when the tribe had moved to the Indian Territory long before I was born.

Everybody had a curious streak in those days. When a tragic train wreck near Henryetta killed a number of blacks, Mom insisted we drive over to see the car in which they had died. It was on a siding and was not badly damaged, because the accident had not been a usual wreck involving an overturned car. Instead, a rush of steam from the damaged locomotive had forced its way into the Jim Crow car and suffocated all of the occupants. I was glad to leave the morbid place, which was thronged with a crowd of whites whose curiosity was hard to understand.

Far more interesting to me was Henryetta's "Doughboy" statue straddling the main street. The life-sized bronze statue of an American infantryman in World War I was probably a standard monument, for I recall seeing similar ones in other towns later. But to me it had heroic significance at a time when movies about the war were standard fare in Hollywood. As I mentioned earlier, my favorite game was playing with toy soldiers of that war, and it had been over only a decade when even breakfast cereal manufacturers began capitalizing on our victory over Germany. After finishing a box of corn flakes, I cut out the soldiers printed on the back, the doughboys in khaki and the Germans in red and black (never mind authenticity), and at the five-and-ten stores in Okmulgee, I went first to the toy counters, which always had a good supply of mounted Americans in khaki and grenade-throwing infantrymen. For a quarter I had a squad I played with endlessly on my own version of a French battlefield, digging tiny trenches with a spoon near our garage on Third Street. For a dime I also purchased a lead version of a French 75mm field gun, with a spring mechanism that threw BB pellets a couple of feet. Many heads and arms were shot off by those pellets or the rocks we tossed back and forth, as we relived the supposed glories of the Battle of the Somme. All our impressions of war were very glamorous, and in our serious moments my playmates and I would speculate on whether we would become generals or admirals, always followed by the phrase, "When I grow up." We did not know how hard it would be to grow up, in fact.

❧10❧

Town and Country Entertainment

The infrequent circuses, carnivals, and medicine shows that came to Okemah for two or three days challenged the movie houses as venues for popular entertainment. The carnivals came by truck and usually were held on a vacant lot on West Broadway, where there was room for a Ferris wheel, merry-go-round, a sideshow, several games of chance, and a couple of wagons selling soft ice cream and popcorn. The rides were a nickel, the games of chance a dime, and the sideshows were sometimes as much as a quarter for adults, but I got in for a dime. The sideshows were grim displays of human cast-offs, albino Negroes purported to be "sheep men" from a Pacific island, a tattooed man or woman, the fat lady, the world's tallest man, and other specimens of nature's peculiar twists. One visit was enough to last a lifetime.

The games were ring-toss or baseball throws to knock down wooden milk bottles, and when the deputy sheriffs cooperated, there was a penny toss into plates bearing five cents, ten cents, and the one in the middle one dollar — sums to be awarded *if* your penny stayed in them. I coveted a hideous pug bulldog made of chalk at one of these carnivals and wasted several precious dimes trying to win one. Mom was probably happy I lost.

The merry-go-rounds had wonderful music from a mechanical band consisting of bass and snare drums, a player piano, and cymbals. The horses, tigers, and giraffes were carved of wood and garishly (beautifully, I thought) painted, but the music was what thrilled as we older children spent our nickels on the Ferris wheel. We soared up above the downtown buildings and could see the distant lights of oil leases and cars traveling on U.S. Route 62. Even though we spent the savings of many weeks in an hour or so, we were always excited when a poster first appeared in a store front announcing a coming carnival, and always sad to see the empty grounds strewn with popcorn boxes, crushed cigarette packs, and the usual trash left behind when the carnival moved on.

As the depression deepened, city officials tried to discourage traveling shows from coming into Okemah by charging a high fee for a one-day operating license. One year local officials did not allow the carnival to visit at all, the reason being, as the *Leader* explained, cash needed to keep the local economy moving would be lost if a carnival or circus were permitted to operate during depression times. This was my first encounter with what I regarded as unnecessary governmental interference in citizens' lives.

Nevertheless, a few circuses stopped occasionally for a day and night performance, and for most boys the event created much excitement. One circus sent out an advance man who plastered telephone poles and barns with pictures and promises of a street parade at noon down Broadway. The big day came, the streets were lined with spectators, but no band, wagons, or clowns had appeared after thirty minutes or so. Then a truck came along with an announcer who shouted into a megaphone: "The heat is bad for the animals, the parade has been canceled."

Maybe that was true, because it *was* hot in Okemah in the summer, but our faith had been broken. After this disappointment, I was determined not to pay to see the circus that night. Standing with a crowd of other little boys at the side of the main tent, we waited for an opportunity to slip in under the canvas folds, after some patrolling roustabouts with clubs in their hands had passed by. Timing was everything, and at the right moment I grabbed canvas and went under the tent on all fours. Then a roustabout spotted me and headed my way. The only avenue of escape was an enclosure marked "Ladies." Making a quick decision, I darted into the forbidden area, which may have been occupied or not, for I was moving too fast to notice. I scooted under the canvas fast enough to avoid a whacking on the back side and in seconds reached the neutral ground surrounding the big top. I was so frightened I kept on going to our house, where I lied and told Mom I had been to the circus and didn't think much of it.

That first, unsatisfying encounter with show business was softened by the next big event, a medicine show that came to Okemah amid much publicity for its banjo players and free minstrel program. A stage was erected on West Broadway, and for about ten days a free performance was held each evening, interrupted several times by sales pitches for an elixir said to cure most of mankind's ailments if taken in the proper dosage. To add zest to their stay in Okemah, the pitchmen held a contest to name a "Miss Okemah," who would be recognized for her beauty and for the number of bottles sold to her supporters.

The prettiest teacher in our schools was, by common agreement, a young girl with blonde hair and blue eyes named Miss McCord. I was in love with her, along with half the boys in the elementary school, and one of us entered her name in the "Miss Okemah" contest. The next day she denounced the whole business with tears in her eyes, but our will was firm and we solicited votes for her every night. On the final night, the master of ceremonies declared our teacher the winner and seemed surprised when she did not come on stage to claim her award. Our mirth turned to sadness as he kept asking the "lucky young lady" to come forward, and by the time the evening was over, we were a sorry band of rascals. The lesson I learned, however, stuck with me: When a person says "no," believe her and leave her alone.

My next encounter with stage shows was Bill Slepka's "Hollywood Premiere" at the Crystal Theater, which he had recently purchased. He enlisted a number of talented Okemahans to impersonate Hollywood celebrities at a premiere complete with spotlights; chauffeur-driven automobiles would deliver the make-believe stars to a temporary stage in front of the theater. The event celebrated Slepka's redecoration of the Crystal, which featured a blue sky, some Grecian statuary on either side of the stage, and other touches of elegance. Slepka boasted in the *Leader* that the Crystal was "one of the three theaters in the state of Oklahoma with moving clouds and twinkling stars." Class!

I had watched the theater's transformation because the Dallas crew working there stayed at Mom's hotel, and they let me come and go as the work proceeded. When Slepka announced the amateur night premiere, they persuaded me to enter as the popular child-star, Mickey Rooney. Rooney's trademark garb was a derby hat, oversized shoes, dark shorts, and loud suspenders. He also chewed on a cigar.

Slepka was a first-class showman. With spotlights going, a stream of new cars (not Pierce Arrows, but Fords) brought all the impersonators to the stage. The crowd applauded as each name was announced, and the impersonators made their way to a microphone and greeted the fans. Mom found a derby hat, suspenders, and a rubber cigar for me to chew on, and I rode to the event with a local grocer's son who was dressed as Harpo Marx, with a blonde wig and crushed top hat as his trademarks.

We had a wonderful time, but the thin veneer of the audience's appreciation gave way when a talented local singer took the stage inside. She was trained as a opera signer and had performed in St. Louis, so she was appearing this night as Jeanette MacDonald. Midway in her rendition, some playful but unappreciative souls started throwing pennies onto the stage. She finished her song and headed for the wings, where I saw her dabbing her eyes and vowing not to sing again. The memory of her humiliation stayed in my mind and was sharpened, some months later, when I learned of a greater tragedy from the *Leader* — the lady's young husband had taken his life.

❁

Tragedy was all around us in Okemah. The owner of the local pool hall was a Czech-American who had been horribly burned in an accident involving Public Service Company power lines, which supplied Okemah with electricity. The man was in his early thirties when the accident left him crippled in one leg and with a false hand, which I heard was made of cork.

After the accident, he bought the pool hall with some of his settlement money. Once when I confessed to him my yearning to play pool, he invited me in and showed me the game of "rotation." I was thrilled to see how accurate he was in dispatching the numbered billiard balls, and he gave me quick lessons on keeping one's feet on the floor and striking the cue ball solidly. He even contrived to make the game close, but I knew he was trying to lose and liked him for it.

We hear that pool halls are not the best places to develop character, but as far as I could tell, the Okemah pool hall was a place to spend a dime and stop worrying about the problems of the day for a while. Yes, I saw men go into the back and have a drink of bootleg whiskey, but they did that all over town. And if an occasional fight started there on a Saturday night, so what? I never saw a local policeman go near the place or stop a fight. Such misdemeanors were allowed to play themselves out without interference from the outside, since knives and other weapons were taboo. In those days, guns were used primarily for hunting.

Gambling was frowned upon at church on Sunday, but even as children we took chances with our pennies in Okemah's five-and-dime stores. I usually went to Harkey's on the south side of Broadway, because the clerks were plump, pleasant ladies who knew us all by our first names. A penny bought you a piece of caramel, and if it had a white center, you won a candy bar. In short order most of us regular customers learned that squeezing the ends of the caramel revealed whether it was a plain toffee or had a reinforcing nougat center. That eliminated the element of chance, but the clerks soon caught on to our game and ended the candy bar bonanza by insisting that the piece picked up was the one you bought.

Another form of gambling with candy arose when a candy bar was offered for a nickel with a slip of paper inside, each bearing a president's name. A poster by the candy bars illustrated the prizes to be won for getting three presidents in a row, including a pocket knife with an iridescent handle that seemed worth any sacrifice. In a week's time I had two of the presidents, Harding and Coolidge, and only needed Herbert Hoover to win the coveted knife. Then I kept buying bars with Taft or Harding slips, however, and I was discouraged.

There was absolutely no way to learn which bar contained a Hoover slip, and I was resigned to living life without that beautiful knife. I told Fred, the soda-fountain operator, that I was giving up hope and would be spending my last nickel on something valuable, such as a double-dip ice-cream cone.

"Try just one more time, then quit," he suggested.

Children don't need much encouragement, so I took the next cash that came my way to the drugstore.

"Fred, this is my last chance. Do you think I should even try?"

"Of course. I think you'll get that knife sooner or later," he replied.

Down went the nickel, and then I weighed my chances, touched several bars, and finally selected the fateful one. In truth, I was prepared to unwrap another Harding, but there it was: HERBERT HOOVER. I don't know if Fred was more elated than I was, but he sure gave a loud whoop when I showed him my winning slip.

Then the disappointment — my slip had to be given to the route salesman to claim the prize, and he would not be in Okemah for another week. But seven days passed, and I did get that knife. Mom said that winning the Zenith radio discount and the knife proved that I was born under a lucky star. I wanted to believe her.

❃

The great southern writers tell of learning to write by recording their memories of family conversations they heard in their youth. In searching my memory of the Okemah days, I realized the great paucity of conversation at the Third Street house and in the Broadway Hotel. The talk was mainly about money, or the lack of it, and ways and means of coping with the monthly bills. That was part of the heritage of the depression, of course, but fortunately, as a live-in relative, I had another side of my life where spirited conversations took place. These occurred during my periodic visits to Uncle Boon's farm east of town, when I was invited by one of several aunts to come for a visit and fish in Uncle Boon's stockpond for catfish.

Uncle Boon's unpainted, two-story house, where my sister lived, had a huge kitchen with a wood stove that was always hot. There was no electricity, so the light after nightfall came from kerosene lamps, and there was no telephone, either. The toilet was thirty yards to the rear of the house. A well off the side porch produced water when a metal tube was dropped, and a rope jerked to bring up the valve, then a few healthy tugs brought up a pailful of drinkable water.

Sitting next to the well usually was a churn, with which Aunt Ethel made the butter she sold in town, and some empty Mason jars. During the summer she canned beans, beets, peaches, and apples for use in the fall and winter; all these were placed in a storm cellar that had been dug behind the porch as a refuge in case of a tornado and also as a cool storage area. The roof was made of earth piled on top of galvanized iron sheets almost a foot deep, so that it was always twenty degrees cooler there than on the outside. Wood for Aunt Ethel's cookstove and the parlor fireplace came from the abundant scrub oaks on the half-abandoned farm.

Spring was often chosen as a convenient time for a small family reunion. Then Aunt Ethel would invite her sisters, my aunts Ruby, Kate, and May, for fried chicken and biscuits. I sometimes rode with Ruby's husband out to the farm. On one such occasion I spent the night sleeping on a pallet of quilts until I walked in my sleep and tumbled down the stairs. The clatter woke up the household. Frightened but unhurt, I whimpered an apology, then crawled back to my pallet in my sister's room.

At meals and afterwards, my aunts and uncles would talk about past times with relish. A hand-wound Victrola in the living room had once played such hit songs as "It Ain't Gonna Rain No More," and "Yes, We Have No Bananas," but it finally gave out. Uncle Boon had not bothered to repair it, so the entertainment consisted of conversation about departed friends and family, the low prices of crops, the poor job politicians were doing, and the prospects for improvement in the roads or the economy. Serious discussion of family matters and problems was seldom allowed, so that by listening to them, I learned nothing about how to cope with life; I did learn the value of family unity.

All my aunts were kind women, but Aunt May was my favorite. Her first husband died when he was young and she had remarried, taking for her husband a well-educated eastern gentleman who verged on being an alcoholic. He had graduated from Washington and Lee University and "never amounted to much," finally coming to Oklahoma as a sometime insurance salesman and also a timekeeper on a WPA project. Aunt May's sweet nature was a good antidote for his sour disposition.

One hot summer afternoon, when the conversation lulled as my aunts and uncles became drowsy, I found a bamboo cane pole and some fishing line and proceeded to go fishing alone in the muddy waters of the pond. Plenty of bait was available in the form of earthworms found near the henhouse. After a short interval I felt a tug on my line, the cork went under, and I hauled out a catfish that might have been seven inches long. Taking the catfish off the hook proved to be problem, however, for I managed to hook my hand and allow the fish to get away.

Tears followed, but Aunt May found some rubbing alcohol to pour on the wound, then she ripped up an old, clean sheet and made an impressive bandage. To soothe me even further, she squeezed some orange juice into a glass, chipped ice off the block in Aunt Ethel's icebox, and made me some weak but welcome orangeade. Her concern and kindness set Aunt May apart, for many years thereafter she would remind me of my mishap and her role as the nurse. She made the incident come alive over the years, as it still does when writing about it. Simple acts of kindness can penetrate the mind so deeply that after sixty years a fragment remains in mine as a kind of memorial to Aunt May, who lived until she was ninety-eight.

Aunt Kate was the dominant aunt, and she had the physical presence to back up her booming voice. I had the notion that my other aunts were a little afraid of Aunt Kate, for she was frank to the point of insult in many conversations. She helped Mom during the pipeliners' boom, for she was a cook of great ability, and she left Okemah with my Uncle Chris, when he took a job in Seminole County, as a deputy sheriff. Several years later, he was shot and killed in Seminole when making an arrest in a car-theft case. I had not liked Uncle Chris since the day he arrested Pop, but I loved Aunt Kate for her booming voice and endless optimism. Her vigilance in seeing that her husband's killer was not released on parole gave her life a new purpose, and as the years passed, we knew little of her vicissitudes except that the killer was still in the state penitentiary and Aunt Kate was working hard to keep him there.

My sister was only a baby when our family broke up, but when she was six, the lure of town brought her to the Third Street house on Saturday, and we would often go to the movies. Our favorites were Laurel and Hardy comedies, with a vigorous replay of the action later when we bought ice-cream cones and went back to the front porch, where she waited for a ride back to the farm. The cash outlay was small, a dime for the show and a nickel for ice cream, but Aunt Ethel met all expenses with semi-suffering. She brought in eggs, cream, and chickens to exchange for coffee, flour, sugar, and perhaps a little extra cash, and she made most of their clothes on her treadle Singer sewing machine, from yard goods bought at the Creek Trading Company store until a cousin went to work for Penney's. Thereafter, the Rutland clan had a discount.

Because they had no automobile, my sister rode a horse to Mountain Grove school in bad weather, while as a town boy I walked only a few blocks. Sis had a pair of shoes, of the style known as Roman sandals, that she took care to keep shined. The only shoes I remember were a patent-leather pair Mom bought me one Easter. It rained that morning, and when I returned from Sunday school, Mom popped them in the oven to dry. They turned into heavy clumps of leather with the consistency of coal and had to be thrown away. Since the shoes had cost two dollars, it was a small tragedy; Mom, who was superstitious anyway, recalled that Easters were bad times in our family because my father had died on Easter Sunday. I liked the Easter egg hunts in the churchyard and tried to reassure her that good things happened on Easter too. The little Easter bunny Pop had found for me as a pet, however, only lasted one day. He was buried with appropriate ceremonies, and I tried to forget the Easter "jinx" that seemed to overshadow our family.

❧ 11 ❧

Mixing Dreams and Prayers

Radio became much more popular in America in the early 1930s, as the technology improved and static was eliminated. Also, President Roosevelt took to the air to explain the nation's problems, and many listened to his confident voice tell us that things could be a lot worse. Mom was not a radio fan, so I did not listen to Amos and Andy at home, like many of my peers. On one occasion I heard Roosevelt's voice when visiting the Palace Drug Store. The pharmacist was a tall, ungainly man who was often consulted, when doctors were not available, for a temporary remedy. I picked up a stopgap remedy for Mom and stayed to listen to the speech. When it ended, the drugstore crowd seemed to approve of what the president had said.

A far more dramatic radio broadcast than the depression news or Roosevelt's remedies was the Lindbergh kidnapping case, which bridged a gap in communications. Most people remember where they were when some significant historical event took place, and my first such memory involved the Lindbergh kidnapping in 1932.

Lindbergh was still America's hero when the news flashed out of New Jersey that his baby son had been kidnapped. Everybody knew who Lindy was — the tousle-headed hero who had conquered space and time. The nation was shocked by the first news announcement, and even in Okemah, "extra" editions of the local newspaper told the latest developments, right up to the final tragic denouement when the baby's body was discovered. In my memory, this was the last time when radio still competed with newspapers; a newsboy could run down the street yelling, "Extra! Extra! Lindbergh Baby's Body Found!" and customers would emerge from homes and stores to spend a nickel for the special edition. After the Lindbergh case, I recall no other event that had such an impact or was considered newsworthy enough to merit a "extra." Besides, the newsrooms of radio stations were becoming more aggressive, with special newsbreaks interrupting broadcasts. When people heard of a catastrophe, they headed for their radio sets instead of the front porch to await a special newspaper edition.

Gossip also played a part of the local news scene. One spring day, headed for the Palace, I noticed a car parked outside it with the two occupants having some lunch. After slowing down, I realized the man was Jack Dempsey, former heavyweight champion of the world, munching his sandwich like any mortal. I flew back to the house to tell Mom, and she wanted to know lady's identity. That meant a trip back to the drugstore, where the excited clerks were discussing the big event. The lady was Estelle Taylor, Dempsey's current wife and former movie personality, and they were in Okemah because, informed gossips told me, Dempsey was on a barnstorming tour of the country, refereeing matches for a handsome fee.

Why had I not found a piece of paper and asked Dempsey for an autograph? I bewailed the lost opportunity, for Jack Dempsey was the most famous person I had ever seen, but his reputation was simply too much for a shy youngster to handle.

Another case of severe self-reproach involved the

poet, Edwin Markham. I found an item in the *Leader* announcing that the famous Markham, who wrote the popular poem "The Man with the Hoe," would be in Okemah to speak at the First Baptist Church, for reasons not clear to me. But I was old enough to realize this was a significant event, and I made preparations to attend. When I reached the church that evening, however, it was empty, except for a custodian.

"Isn't Edwin Markham supposed to be here tonight?" I asked.

Without looking up, the man kept sweeping the floor. "That was last night," he said.

I turned pink with embarrassment and thought I learned a lesson to check the date of the newspaper I was reading. It would be pleasant to report that such an incident has never occurred since — but it wouldn't be true.

❀

Pneumonia was a killing malady that often defeated doctors in the twenties and thirties. My father had died of pneumonia, so it was a dreaded word in my vocabulary. Thus when our prettiest schoolteacher, Miss Brass, was stricken with the disease in the winter of 1932, I began to worry. This lovely young girl, only twenty-four, was a beauty I compared to the movie star, Sylvia Sidney, in both her appearance and appeal. When we learned that she was losing ground fast, I asked Mom why God let good people have so much pain. Her answers did not reassure me.

Within a week, the *Leader* carried the sad story that Miss Brass had died, and her funeral would be held in the First Baptist Church. All her pupils were upset, and I was determined to go to the first funeral in my memory. The church was full, and there was a great outpouring of sympathy for her parents. When we filed by the casket, I was struck by her quiet beauty, and my heart was still full of questions about the justice of such a sad event. Outside of my father's death, nothing jolted me so much as the thought of Miss Brass's tragic demise. The old saw that "the good die young" did not seem to be a fit explanation, then or now.

Saturdays were the busy days in Okemah, for the farmers came to town to buy on credit their coffee, sugar, and flour, and trading cream or eggs for partial credit. The Jewel Theater owners had installed a loudspeaker system that blared most of the day and into the night, mainly country music, and the senseless din preyed on my mind as I contrasted my dream world in Tulsa with the real world around me. The dust storms continued, the weather was depressing with its continuous days of ninety-five-degree heat and little rain. After school ended in May 1934, I feared there was no escape from my predicament. Would I never be able to live with my mother?

The Okemah experience would end some day, I knew, but looking ahead I saw that high school was not so far away. Would I be going to Okemah High School or Tulsa Central? I was tired of being teased by playmates for wearing the tan cotton shorts my mother gave me; anything from my mother was held sacred, but in Okemah, shorts were considered "sissy" by all who wore overalls, so I had to be persuaded that Tulsa boys wore them all the time and *never* wore overalls. The day-to-day monotony of the hotel was becoming harder to take, and it seemed the only changes were the seasons and the weather.

Except during the school year, I had fewer playmates after we moved to the Broadway. My loneliness was exaggerated by constant longing to be with my mother. I read the Tulsa newspapers with care, hoping to find an excuse to visit her — a circus, a fireworks display — anything out of the ordinary to make my pleas more reasonable.

The Crystal Theater that once seemed so magnificent wasn't all that appealing after seeing the Ritz in Tulsa. The Ritz was my idea of what a palace should look like, for it had not only a ceiling full of twinkling stars but also a grand staircase to the balcony and side wall filled with Greek gods and goddesses. After the movie the lights came up and an organ rose in front of the stage. For thirty minutes a jovial organist led the audience through a series of sing-alongs, with the "bouncing ball" guiding us through the lyrics. This was big-time stuff.

I also missed the evening rides "to cool off" that ended at a watermelon stand, where a dime bought a full-length slice of ice-cold melon. Mr. Degen, my mother's beau, sometimes took us to the Good Humor ice cream shop, where the flavors were not just ordinary chocolate, vanilla, and strawberry; the Tulsa emporium had a long list of exotic flavors like chocolate chip, pistachio, or my favorite, banana.

And then there was Swan Lake, not the ballet but the small lake near one of the rooming houses my mother lived in during 1931–1932. The lake had real swans and no fence, so it was possible to walk down to the water and see tadpoles swimming below the surface. Taken altogether, in my vision Tulsa seemed like a paradise on earth.

A bright spot occurred one afternoon after going to a movie at the Crystal. Emerging from the theater, I smelled a strange scent — rain! People were laughing from under the awnings on Broadway, for maybe this was a sign the drought had broken. The hot weather returned with the bright sun, however, before the afternoon ended. Still, the precious rainbow reminded us that nothing lasts forever — not even a drought.

I kept busy searching the alleys for empty bottles that could be returned for a deposit or finding bits of scrap lead or copper to sell. At the junk yard I realized how pitiful my efforts were when the owner's son hinted I was bothering them needlessly.

"Your copper is only worth a dime," he said. "Why don't you save up enough to bring in at least a quarter's worth?"

The point was well made, so much so that I never tried to sell him scrap metal again. I tried to revive my "circus" of celluloid animals, but no pipeline crews were around and the few tenants in Mom's boardinghouse had no time for my pitiful display of animals. There were no bricks to clean, either. The country was in a depression and so was a twelve-year-old youngster who walked the streets in search of an idea.

The premium on ingenuity grew during the depression as dollars became harder and harder to find. The city of Okemah felt the pinch and resorted to issuing script to pay desperately poor men one dollar a day to clean streets, repair sidewalks, and avoid the out-and-out dole. The *Leader* said "about a dozen" men and their families would benefit from the city's effort to combat unemployment. Large paper bills with spaces for fifty-cent stamps were paid out in lieu of cash, while each user affixed a one-cent stamp in each space until all of them were filled. The city treasurer sold the stamps, and when fifty had been used, the scrip could be redeemed for a silver half-dollar. The novelty of the idea wore off, but Mom bought her stamps along with most of the merchants on Broadway, and all the scrip thus issued eventually came back into the city coffers, fully redeemed.

God seemed to have created "hard times" to make boys go fishing — a time to forget conditions at home by watching a bobbing cork. That summer, after investing a few pennies on an Eagle Claw hook, I often dug up some earthworms, borrowed a bamboo pole from Pop, and with my kite string and pocket knife would head for Rock Creek south of town. I hitched a wagon ride, and in about an hour I was five miles from town, all alone, and ready to catch catfish.

Rock Creek was a spring-fed stream that had a few deep holes around the bridge on the county section-line road. During the summer of 1934, it was my place for soul-searching. It seemed the depression was never going to end; Mom was crying at night about the unpaid bills, and the number of tenants and boarders was decreasing. The best bedroom, with Mom's favorite bed and dresser from the Third Street house, rented for seventy-five cents a night and was usually unoccupied. The overnight customers, some without luggage, paid fifty cents for a room with double bed. A night clerk had been employed at the outset, but his job eventually was eliminated because the rental income didn't cover his salary of three dollars a week.

Money seemed to control everything, and everyone was desperately trying to get more. One promoter, whom I knew from my few escapades in the pool hall, was a man of about thirty named Buck Martin. He wore his straw hat at a jaunty angle and reportedly made a living by sponsoring Saturday night dances in the second floor ballroom of a former furniture store, now closed by the depression. Martin's great coup was bringing the famous Bob Wills and his Texas Playboys band to Okemah. The coming event was announced on KVOO, and the night of the dance I joined a group of youngsters listening to the band from car-fender seats on the street below.

I had not heard "San Antonio Rose" before, and it sounded good. As I saw couples going up to the ballroom, I speculated about how much fun it would be when I had a girl and could take her to a big dance — that is, a ballroom where it cost a whole dollar per couple to get in.

Martin had ambition, and his search for real talent became national news for a brief moment. According to news reports, Martin had asked the manager of Paul Whiteman's orchestra if the "King of Jazz" would come to Okemah for a one-hundred-dollar fee. The news story said Whiteman had replied; "For one hundred dollars, I'll send you my piccolo player." It was a good story, although Buck denied it, and for a moment Okemah was in the special spotlight reserved for the culturally barren small towns of America.

❀

My prayers to join my mother increased in intensity, for I saw how bad things were becoming in Okemah. The dream took on a gloss of possibility in the summer of 1933, when my mother told me about a YMCA camp for boys she thought I would like. Since going to the camp meant a trip to see her, I was excited from the first mention until the day I boarded the bus outside the Tulsa YMCA, along with about forty other youngsters carrying duffel bags. All I knew was that the camp cost ten dollars for ten days, including bus fare. Mom heard stories about the camp in Okemah and was skeptical, but she helped me pack a bathing suit made of scratchy wool, my B.V.D. underwear, tennis shoes, and shorts in my tan duffel bag.

The bus trip to Grove, Oklahoma, took about three hours and was full of singing and shouting. I had never been so far away from home before — Okemah was all of 140 miles away — and the combination of adventure and song made the trip seem like the joyride of a lifetime. The hit song was "Pennies from Heaven," which was easy to learn, and by the time our bus reached the camp, we were all good buddies.

Camp Kemp was a new world for me. Situated on a bluff overlooking the Elk River, the camp had perhaps twelve bunkhouses arranged as a square, with a flagpole in the middle and a mess hall located about a hundred yards away. Each cabin had double-decker bunks for eight boys and wooden footlockers for storing clothes. A few boys in every cabin were staying for twenty or thirty days; we who had come for shorter stays were treated as "new boys" but there was no hazing, just supercilious conversation from the holdovers.

We piled off the bus and were assigned a cabin and locker, then assembled in the mess hall for our first meal, on long tables covered with oilcloth and set with places for each cabin's occupants. We quickly learned that spilling iced tea, lemonade, or food on the tables hurt our chances of being selected as the cleanest table — an honor announced after the mealtime inspection by the camp director.

Our cabin counselor, who was all of seventeen or

eighteen, was a high school student signed on for the summer who received room and board as compensation. In 1933, that meant a relieved breadwinner back home, and a counselor was as good as employed at a time when jobs were a rarity. My counselor was also an Eagle Scout, which meant that he knew everything that needed to be known about camping.

My first night was full of excitement as we went to a campfire, sitting on wooden benches arranged in a circle around the fire. We were told of the traditions at Camp Kemp, an officer of the day was chosen for the following day (a great honor, obviously), and the program for tomorrow explained. We sang songs I had not heard before, such as "I Been Working on the Railroad," staggered choruses of "Row, Row, Row Your Boat," and "O, Susannah!" Then we took a trail back to our cabins and stopped off at the latrine, a military term, it seemed, for a bath/toilet house. During the night I started to sob, suffering from what the cabin counselor diagnosed as homesickness; eventually I fell asleep and never felt the pangs again.

The camp director was Max Morrison, a Presbyterian minister. He spoke with authority but kindness each day as he reminded us of the need for cleanliness and caution — careful walking on the paths to avoid snakes or poison ivy was an oft-repeated warning. As for cleanliness, we soon learned how to make our bunk beds, sweep the floor or swab it with a wet mop, and to be ready for each morning's inspection after breakfast. The best-kept cabin for each day was announced at lunch and a special flag placed at the head of the cabin's table. Winning that flag became an object of our desires, and I think our minister-director had to fudge a bit to see that the honor was spread around.

Max Morrison was that kind of guy. He was friendly

and fair, and his wife, who also lived in the director's cabin, became my friend when a boy in my cabin broke his eyeglasses and I stepped on a piece of the glass lodged between the flooring planks. She calmed me down and bandaged the wound with such serenity that I soon tagged after her to and from the mess hall, awaiting some sign of recognition. When she called me "Bobby," I felt accepted in this wondrous place. We spent each morning on a nature trail, or the rifle range, or in a craft shop. I liked the rifle range best, but .22 caliber ammunition was not cheap, perhaps a penny per bullet, so I did not fire on the range as much as I would have liked. I had fifty cents for ten days' spending money, but that had to cover my desire for a Baby Ruth candy bar each evening or some .22 shells for the next day. We bought tickets at the canteen, ten for fifty cents, to be used sparingly for purchases. A companion who bought both a candy bar and package of chewing gum on the same day was regarded as something of a spendthrift.

After lunch we waited an hour, then put on bathing suits and sneakers and walked several hundred yards, winding our way down a wooden staircase along the cliff and taking a trail on the banks of the Elk. The river had a stony bed, so the sneakers had to be worn to prevent cutting one's feet on the rocks.

Since I did not swim, I was careful to walk over a shallow, narrow passage to the swimming area watched by life guards. Although the wool suits were uncomfortable, I think wool was used because it kept its shape in those days before synthetics, and made more sensible bathing gear. I made little progress in swimming, however, because the heavy suits and sneakers made it more difficult with all that weight to carry. One memorable afternoon a recent rain had caused the river to rise slightly, and as we were returning in a narrow line across the shallow passage, the current swept me off the path. I went down once, then twice, and was about to yell for help when I found a dangling tree branch to clutch and work my way to shore. My pride almost cost me dearly.

The food in our mess hall was not so important as the conversation; we traded stories about the day's activities, the rewards and the failures. We could choose our daily programs, and because hunting for arrowheads required no cash outlay, I often opted for these hikes through ploughed cornfields after rains. The nearby farmers did not object as long as we were careful to walk down the rows, looking for arrowheads revealed after a shower. Nearly every day I found one or two and was impressed by the Indians' workmanship. Most were missing their tips, which had been broken off hundred of years earlier, so we were told, by Indians hunting rabbits, squirrels, or deer. I kept these treasures and showed them off back in Okemah as tangible mementos of my camping days.

As we became better acquainted, my cabinmates and I talked about our homes, and I soon realized I was the only boy in our group who had no father and didn't live with my mother. Everybody else came from a home with mothers, fathers, sisters, and brothers. This was brought home acutely on the Sunday when my mother and her friend visited camp and had lunch with us. All boys were asked to introduce their parents, and when it came my turn, I had to think quickly. I was almost quaking as I rose to say that my visitors were "my mother and our friend, Mr. Degen." It was a crisis met and solved, and mother complimented me later on the way I handled it.

After supper we usually played softball or took walks until dusk, when we assembled at the campfire. Even in hot weather the evening fire felt good, and as it burned down to embers, a counselor would often tell a ghost story to send us back to our cabins in mock terror. Cabins also arranged to do programs on certain nights, for which we made up skits, a new experience for me. One skit involved a long story that ended with a victim rapidly repeating the names of three "great Indian tribes" — "the Owah, the Tagoos, and Siam." When repeated loudly, the phrase produced an uproar and a blush for the unwary victim. The innocence and laughter deeply impressed me.

Another memorable incident concerned a near tragedy. After lights out at camp, the counselors would meet and carry on until midnight, either driving into Grove or going down to the Elk River bridge. We learned one morning that a counselor given to braggadocio had dived off the bridge at a shallow spot and been knocked unconscious. Fortunately his friends realized what had happened and quickly brought him back to safety, but at lunch that day we were warned, in Morrison's harshest manner, against jumping off the bridge.

At the end of ten days I was saddened by the prospect of returning to Okemah, but once back at the hotel I talked for hours about my adventures, the songs learned, the people I had met, and Max Morrison in particular. Mom laughed, saying that for ten dollars I *should* have had a good time and apparently I had. I secretly began planning to return in 1934, and in letters scribbled to my mother I dropped hints that were not subtle.

The fact that she spent ten dollars to send me to Camp Kemp left me with the impression that my mother was not so financially strained in Tulsa and that somehow things were much better in the city than in Okemah. In 1929 she had left Okmulgee to work in linens and piece goods at the Brown-Dunkin Department Store. Her starting salary for six-days work was six dollars a week, Monday through Saturday, but her salesmanship impressed an executive there, and she was made an assistant to the linen department buyer. After five years, she now made fifteen dollars a week, and by making out a budget, which included an apartment at thirty dollars a month, she figured she could bring me to Tulsa by September 1934.

I have no doubt that my mother also perceived a certain unwholesomeness in the living conditions at the Broadway Hotel, and from her own experiences in 1918 and 1919, she had an undeserved contempt for Okemah's public schools. My letters inquiring about Camp Kemp for the 1934 session brought the joyous news in the spring that I could go back for twenty days that summer. I showed her letter to Mom, whose reaction was that "Bea must be doing real well if she can spend twenty dollars on a boy's camping trip."

A black moment, amid all the good news, came one day that spring when I walked up to the mill to see my grandfather and found him in a drunken state. I told him the news about returning to camp, which made no impression on him at all. He began to ramble about my mother, my father's death, and then suddenly said; "It wouldn't surprise me if Bea jumped into the river." I knew enough to understand what Pop was saying in his drunkenness — that my mother might commit suicide. It was a terrifying thought, but I realized he was despondent himself, so I returned to the hotel and asked Mom what had caused him to make such an awful prediction. She consoled me by saying Pop was so drunk he didn't realize what he was saying. I hoped and prayed she was right.

Apparently, my mother realized that the family situation in Okemah was deteriorating to a desperate point in the lives of her father and stepmother. This is speculation from hindsight, of course, for at the time, even though I sensed the strain between them, I understood little about relationships that went back a decade or more. I *was* aware of an intense desire to be with my mother full time, however, and my nightly prayer always ended with the request that God allow me to live with her in Tulsa. The urgency of those prayers increased after I returned from camp the summer of 1933; I longed to leave Okemah so much that I found fault with many things I had once held dear. In the movies I noticed the smells of tobacco juice and body odors, and the recorded country music played by the Jewel Theater's loudspeaker all day Saturday suddenly sounded tasteless and corny. I hated my overalls and wondered what it would be like to wear a suit on Sundays. The rats marauding in the dark hotel kitchen, which I had once accepted as part of the whole scheme of things, suddenly became a menace.

And I began to have cavities in my teeth. Because Mom did not brush her teeth, she had never taught me to brush mine; not until I went to summer camp did I learn about daily brushing. My ignorance of oral hygiene upset my mother; and she sent me to a Tulsa dentist, who shook his head and wondered aloud how such a young boy could have such bad teeth. No dentist in Okemah was prepared to handle the gold inlays needed to save me from extensive permanent damage. I knew these involved a good deal of money, so for the time being the problem of recurring toothaches was left unresolved.

As worrisome as the crumbling molars was the prospect of beginning another school year in Okemah. My youthful optimism was unquenchable, however; I was full of faith and knew that in time my prayers would be answered. The only question was when?

Returning from a dismal fishing trip to Rock Creek, I found Mom sitting in her bedroom crying. I wanted to console her and asked the cause of her tears?

"Your mother has written me, asking how I would feel about letting you move to Tulsa," she said.

The next minute was probably the happiest of my life. I knew that Mom would not try to prevent my moving, no matter how much she would miss me. My joy counterbalanced Mom's tears. I could be ready to move the next day and tried to say so diplomatically, as I assured her that we would always love each other and that she could visit me in Tulsa any time. Mom knew how much it meant to me and simply told me I would be moving there in time for the fall school term, around September 1. Then more tears fell, and I felt so sorry for her that I scraped in my peanut-shaped bank and found fifteen cents.

Within minutes I was in Harkey's five-and-ten, telling the joyous news to the lady clerk I knew there. I added that I needed a present for Mom, because she was sad and crying. We considered a number of options, and I finally settled on a ceramic swan, clearly labeled on the bottom "Made in Japan," next to the fifteen-cent price tag. She wrapped the swan in tissue paper, and I flew back to the Broadway Hotel with my prize. Mom was still sniffling when I gave her my gift, and the tears continued as she placed it with other treasures on her dresser. I wouldn't realize for many years just how much my little swan meant to her.

The next few weeks dragged by, but now I had a target date, and I must have told half the population of Okemah that I was headed for the big city. It never occurred to me that my sister might also be coming along, but via the family grapevine I heard that my mother could afford only a one-bedroom apartment. Ruth Ann would be sent for later.

Mom's attitude changed somewhat, for she realized how happy I had become. No more need to visit Rock Creek or hunt for scrap metal behind garages. And I disdained the overalls that had been my standard uniform for the past six years. In Tulsa, I was told, schoolboys wore knickers and took baths every night — another change ahead because my weekly bath was on Saturday mornings.

The end of August finally came, and although the thermometer registered over ninety degrees, to me it was a springlike day. Mr. Degen, my mother's steady boy-friend, drove down by prearrangement and helped me pack my B.V.D.s, socks, one pair of corduroy knickers, a sweater or two, a few shirts, and my cigar box full of treasures, which now included the arrowheads I had found at Camp Kemp the previous summer. A tearful farewell followed with Mom, Pop, and the new man in Mom's life. Then we were off, loaded into Mr. Degen's 1932 Chevrolet with its sporty rumble seat. But I left behind sadness as I looked back at Mom and waved goodbye. My days in Okemah were over.

I liked Mr. Degen and he seemed to like me. Rolling along Route 66 between Sapulpa and Tulsa, he made me a wager. "I'll bet you a nickel I see the Philtower on the Tulsa skyline before you do," he said as we came closer to our destination. Somehow I won that bet, possibly because he let me win or maybe because I was so eager to see my new hometown.

Mom soon divorced my grandfather and went with her friend to live in Dallas. Mr. Lawson had talked to me before I left, in a kind of man-to-man fashion, and told me he was leaving the insurance business to become a barber and might move back to Texas. When Mom died in 1970, I went back to her home and found on her dresser a picture of her around 1928, wearing a fox fur-piece wrapped around her plump figure. The only other item on the dresser was the ceramic swan, yellowing from age but still intact.

With a feeling akin to reverence I picked it up and turned it over. On the bottom, next to the "Made in Japan" label, was the fifteen-cent price tag. In all her moves from Okemah to Dallas to Miami, Oklahoma, and finally to Joplin, she had treasured that swan for thirty-six years as a memento of her love for a little boy.

Epilogue

My beautiful mother rescued me in 1934, but she kept Mr. Degen waiting for six more years. He lived in a rooming-house not far from our apartment house, the Morningside Apartments, until mother finally agreed to marry him in 1940, when they bought a home on the then-outskirts of Tulsa, at 25th Street and Lewis Avenue. She became a buyer at Brown-Dunkin in 1936. Once she attended a P.T.A. meeting at Horace Mann Junior High where the students came with their parents. With her brown curly hair, brown eyes, and winsome manner, I was so proud of how nice she looked, and prouder the next day when my classmates told me what a pretty mother I had. I knew that, but I was glad others noticed her beauty. At five feet, three inches, she was one inch taller than Mr. Degen. He had a shock of wavy, grayish hair, thick eyeglasses, and a firm handshake. He sold insurance for the New York Life Insurance Company, and impressed on me the importance of looking into a person's eyes while offering a *firm* handshake.

Perhaps my mother's Presbyterian background was the reason she took so long to marry this wonderful Jewish man from New York's East Side. We never discussed it. In time, growing out of a silly incident, I took to calling him "Mack." Until his death on his sixty-ninth birthday in 1963, he was always "Mack," and I said it with great affection.

Ruth Ann, my sister, never came to live with us in Tulsa. Because she was only a year old when she was taken in by my aunt and uncle, they seemed more like her real parents, and she chose to stay with them. After graduating from Okemah high School, she married a local sweetheart and now lives in Oklahoma City.

Pop moved to Shawnee shortly after I left Okemah, and for a while he was the caretaker of a rich man's house there. He never discussed his former wife but wrote often, mainly about going hunting with my two cousins who lived in Shawnee. During World War II, while I was stationed briefly in Norman, I hitchhiked over to see him and was discouraged by his rather mean life-style. He was living on the $17 provided by the old age assistance plan and the monthly check my mother sent him. I pressed a few dollar bills on him but should have given more.

I saw Pop only once or twice after that, and I think I was somewhat ashamed of how he had let himself go. Looking back, I have mixed feelings still, with some regret that I didn't offer more assistance in his declining years. At some point he bought a motor scooter, and one snowy day early in 1959, he took it and his .22 rifle to shoot a rabbit or two. Skidding into an intersection, he was struck by a car and died in a Tulsa hospital two weeks later. He was eighty-six.

Mom left the Broadway Hotel late in 1934 and moved with her friend Lloyd Lawson to Dallas, where he did open a barber shop. She obtained a divorce from Pop, then she and Lawson married and moved to Miami, Oklahoma. She wrote me often, and when her husband died during World War II, she moved again, this time to Joplin, Missouri, where she bought a small hotel. She remarried and once more became a widow. She was living there in 1970 when she died. She left no will, and as her stepgrandchild, under Missouri law, I was entitled to none of her possessions; however, her legal heir (the son of the last husband) gave me one of her hand-painted plates — my favorite one with the turkey gobbler and her "C.E.N." signature. At her graveside rites in a Joplin cemetery, the only attendants were a Presbyterian minister, my sister and her husband, and me.

My mother died in 1981. She never fully recovered from Mr. Degen's death, yet she tried to make a life for herself through volunteer work and visits to her grandchildren.

As for me, life in Tulsa was not a disappointment. My years there were a kind of heaven on earth. The photographs accumulated from that time over some sixty years remind me of those years of transition, and occasionally I take the browning pictures from their attic storage place and relive the good days again in one corner of my mind. The mystic chords of memory encourage us to hold on to the moments when life was full of everyday pleasures and hope, as our youth always should be. And I am eternally grateful, because all those good things came together for me in the magic year of 1934.